An Outdoor Sporting Life

An Outdoor Sporting Life

*A Celebration of
Heartland Hunting,
Fishing, Friendship,
and Landscape*

SCOTT IRWIN

iUniverse®

AN OUTDOOR SPORTING LIFE
A Celebration of Heartland Hunting, Fishing, Friendship, and Landscape

iUniverse books may be ordered through booksellers or by contacting:

iUniverse
1663 Liberty Drive
Bloomington, IN 47403
www.iuniverse.com
1-800-Authors (1-800-288-4677)

Because of the dynamic nature of the Internet, any web addresses or links contained in this book may have changed since publication and may no longer be valid. The views expressed in this work are solely those of the author and do not necessarily reflect the views of the publisher, and the publisher hereby disclaims any responsibility for them.

Any people depicted in stock imagery provided by Thinkstock are models, and such images are being used for illustrative purposes only.
Certain stock imagery © Thinkstock.

ISBN: 978-1-4917-7104-4 (sc)
ISBN: 978-1-4917-7103-7 (e)

Library of Congress Control Number: 2015911991

Print information available on the last page.

iUniverse rev. date: 08/26/2015

For my family—immediate and extended—and a lifetime of outdoor sporting mentors, especially the late Dale Hogan, and many other outdoor companions who have taught with example, farsighted ethics, humor, and patience and by leading me to new thresholds of experience.

Contents

Foreword

More than a few individuals expressed disappointment and angst when Professor Scott Irwin (aka Masche Field) informed readers of The Emporia Gazette that he was taking an indefinite hiatus after four decades of writing his Flint Hills Outdoors column to write this book. It is now my joy to tell his loyal followers that their pain was not in vain. This compilation will reward readers with entertaining and informative yarns about the rich natural world and the people of the Great Plains told in his easy, familiar style.

I first met Scott nearly 30 years ago when he asked me to provide a forecast for the upland bird-hunting season. I rubbed my crystal ball and prognosticated, using the most reliable survey data available. To my pleasure, Scott's article was spot-on. He accurately conveyed the information in a clear, concise and understandable manner. I have since come to know him as not only a beloved and almost fanatically followed columnist but an admired educator, an accomplished outdoorsman (exceptional wing shot), a gentle family man, a community leader, and the living definition of the word *credible*.

Scott has applied all his skills, knowledge and humor (homespun and wry) to stories that capture a lifetime of outdoor sporting activities on the prairie. These stories are organized in a logical progression of seasons, coincidentally much like Aldo Leopold's "A Sand County Almanac" (1949). Scott's ubiquitous appetite for all things outdoors and sporting, such as hunting, fishing, trekking, birding and spending time with family, friends and neighbors, will appeal to a wide range of readers with varying skills and interests. His background as a teacher and a scientist, and his passion for writing about the natural world, will leave readers checking their calendars for the next opportunity to get outdoors and wishing they could join him on his forays afield.

Like Leopold, Scott is a university professor, so his stories would be expected to offer lessons. In that regard, three themes regularly occur. First, there is his respect and appreciation for the farmers and ranchers who are the stewards of the land and who provide habitat and access. Next, he reflects on the therapeutic and often cathartic effects of spending as much time as possible outdoors. For some of us, Scott included, this is more than a temporary escape; it is a necessity. Last, he offers the message that above all, outdoors people should act as models for those who share their passion for outdoor activities and, just as important, for those who don't. He accomplishes this without being judgmental or preachy, instead conducting himself in ways that make him the consummate outdoor companion. (I hope my bird dog doesn't read this.)

Asked why I moved to Kansas twice, I have usually answered with something about how I enjoy the landscape, the natural resources and the people. However, I have never felt I was able to make my justification for moving back satisfactorily understood—until now. This book is the answer! It clearly captures and concisely describes what I value about living in the Flint Hills. Moreover, it does this in a much more entertaining and insightful manner than I could ever hope to duplicate. In closing, I thank the longtime followers of Scott's column for their patience during his absence, and of course I'm grateful to the newspaper editor who encouraged Scott to write his first article 40-plus years ago. That editor unleashed a lifelong passion for explaining what many of us feel is uniquely important about living in the Great Plains, culminating in this thoroughly enjoyable and uplifting book.

Kevin E. Church, Ph.D., conservation biologist and sawyer

Acknowledgments

I must extend my gratitude to those listed below, without whom publication of this book might have remained an unfulfilled pipe dream.

- First and foremost, to decades of readers for their respect and passion for their own outdoor sporting lives and for their constructive feedback, great patience and occasional encouragement concerning my writing about our shared love of nature.

- To Christopher White Walker, editor and publisher of The Emporia Gazette, for encouraging the reprinting in book form of edited revisions of outdoor sporting columns originally published in the Gazette from 1972 to 1973 and from 1982 to 2014.

- To the late Ray Call and to subsequent editors of the Gazette who appreciated and respected the level of interest in hunting, fishing and general outdoor recreation among the readers of their regional daily newspaper.

- To Cheryl Unruh, author of "Flyover People" and "Waiting on the Sky," for reading enough of my outdoor columns to encourage patient editing and assembly of a collection of those columns in a book manuscript.

- To Jerilynn Henrikson for using her retired English teacher's keen editorial eye, the enthusiasm generated by her successful publication of books for young readers, including the most recent, "Teddy: The Ghost Dog of Red Rocks," and the momentum from both to see the potential of "An Outdoor Sporting Life."

- To Dr. Kevin Church, retired wildlife conservationist, keen observer of all things natural, and a great friend with whom I'd follow a pair of "developing" bird dogs anywhere.

- To neighbor, friend, exceptional outdoorsman, and camp-chef-without-equal Bill Hartman for introducing me to float-tube fishing and for offering me a much-needed reintroduction to his unique approaches to fly fishing.

- To Adam Sergeant and other staff at Emporia State University's information technology center for performing computer debugging miracles that made deadlines less stressful.

- To Deborah Mulsow and her remarkable staff at Emporia State's copy center for superb word processing and printing during the middle stages of this book project.

- To the members of the iUniverse book publishing staff, who served as my support team throughout this book project.

- To Dr. Sophie Thayer, spouse, friend and patient supporter throughout months of reviewing, selecting and editing.

Scott Irwin

Introduction

"An Outdoor Sporting Life" is a collection selected from 40-plus years of outdoor sporting columns published in The Emporia Gazette and a few other Kansas and Texas newspapers. Some I originally wrote under the pen name Masche Field.

My motivation has been simple and direct: to share with readers—young and old, outdoor novice and veteran—stories, essays and confessions from a rural hometown life of small-water fishing, small-game hunting, and wing-shooting adventures that are still unfolding across a patchwork landscape of tallgrass prairie, shortgrass plains, row-crop uplands, and life-changing friendships.

Articles included in the collection are sequenced according to the seasons of the year in which they were written and published. Below the title on the first page of each chapter, I have provided the month and the year of original publication for added perspective.

Readers can observe celebrations and lamentations over many years of fishing and gaming, beginning in the late winter of January, February and early March and continuing through spring, summer and autumn to the early-winter outings of November and December.

Those with specialized interests can zero in on specific topics: spring and summer invasions of farm ponds and creek pools for pan fish and black bass or the pursuit of doves, prairie chickens and sharp-tail grouse in autumn. Readers can accompany me and a rotating cadre of remarkably tolerant Flint Hills cohorts as we chase game birds across Kansas, Nebraska and South Dakota, and they can laugh at and with me and my old West Texas friends during our annual pheasant hunt across West Kansas. They can also enjoy samplings from decades of up-and-down cycles with quail.

These pieces invite readers to step back and experience what a legendary outdoor tale spinner, the late Gene Hill, called "just being there," a tiny strand in the all-encompassing web of an outdoor sporting life.

Scott Irwin

Part One: Late-Winter Overview

In good years, the weeks of January, February and early March may be filled with good upland hunting and early ice-out pond fishing; in lean years, we may spend those weeks comforting ourselves with memories of better years and monitoring the land in search of any and all promises of a better cycle in the coming year.

Perhaps we fill some of that time investing in our friendships with those faithful stewards of the land: the farmers and ranchers whose generous sharing of their natural resources makes our outdoor sporting life possible. Maybe we refocus our time, energy and other resources to work with wildlife conservation groups so they, in turn, can help the keepers of the land maintain or enhance wildlife habitat.

The author steadfastly contends all that went into harvesting these birds is worth repeating. (See chapter 4.)

Chapter 1

Thoughts on Wildlife in Winter

January 2011

It's becoming a challenge to refill the six nylon-mesh thistle-seed bags hanging from randomly selected limbs of an ash tree outside our kitchen window. Neighborhood finches can empty them in short order. And near the trunk of that tree, there's a pair of shoulder-high canister-type feeders that we are constantly filling as doves, cardinals, chickadees, juncos and an occasional acrobatic squirrel gobble up a mixture of safflower and sunflower seeds.

Since the snow arrived, we've enjoyed a three-ring avian circus: finches all over the mesh bags; the usual variety of winter seed eaters mentioned above draining the canisters; and a diverse flock of ground feeders scratching and pecking at the gazillions of seeds that sprinkle down from the feeders and the thistle bags.

With numb fingers I came teetering down the stepladder a little after noon on Wednesday, having filled all those feeders and bags for the third time in a 10-day span. I felt a renewed respect for how Great Plains wildlife—game and nongame—cope with winter.

For most wildlife populations, winter is a season of stress, bringing freezing temperatures, reduced food supplies and higher mortality rates. The snow, ice, and wind chills of the past week make survival difficult. Our resident and transient species of outdoor critters can be hit hard by extended periods of winter stress. Heavy blankets of ice and snow may cover seeds and other food sources that provide life-sustaining energy. Coupled with high winds and extremely low temperatures, such conditions can cause widespread mortality.

Winter mortality is a fact of life for wildlife communities. And, as contradictory as it might seem, harvesting of some game species through carefully regulated hunting can help stabilize populations at optimum levels by decreasing the numbers of critters competing for a limited food supply.

The Critical Factor

What else can we do to help wildlife cope with Great Plains winters? Generations of research on the ebb and flow of wildlife populations— those in hometown backyards and across the patchwork quilts of our agricultural landscape—consistently lead to the same pivotal issue: the carrying capacity of habitat.

Farmers and ranchers who manage their land to include crucial winter food and cover for wildlife know this. They plant small strips or patches of food plots; they seed native, warm-season grasses (think: bluestem— big and little, indian grass, grama grass) into those odd erodible corners, edges and waterways across their fields; they leave a few rows of standing grain or grain stubble at intervals along scattered edges of cropland. A weedy fencerow or ditch here, a brushy corner there may not look like Better Homes and Gardens, but they can spell the difference between death and survival for wildlife.

Those who live in cities and towns can help. Any homeowner can make winter easier for wildlife by establishing trees, shrubs, feeders and other improvements to backyard habitat.

Winter is a stressful time for wild animals, but with proper management and cooperation among landowners, wildlife professionals, hunters, wildlife conservation groups, kitchen-window birdwatchers, and other concerned citizens, we can establish and maintain optimum wildlife habitat.

Chapter 2

Late-Winter (Quail) Food for Thought

January 1991

On a dull, overcast morning earlier this week, what started out as a two-hour quail hunt to celebrate the thawing of our recent icy ground cover unfolded into a graphic lesson in game-bird nutrition. Perhaps you have read the bioenergetics articles published in recent years by state fish-and-game agencies and wildlife conservation support groups and organizations, maybe even some of the advanced graduate research being done at several of the nation's leading land-grant universities with agricultural extension and wildlife management programs. However, a firsthand experience sure brought the issue of game-bird diets closer to home.

I'll spare you a lengthy account of spectacular dog work and wing shooting and stick to the important facts: we harvested four quail from a covey of 15 to 20 birds, flushed at the edge of milo (grain sorghum) stubble left standing through the winter on the east side of a neighbor's farm. An hour later, we took four more quail from a covey of 12 to 15 birds we'd seen at intervals through the previous summer while driving to and from town. The birds would be working their way back and forth across a familiar location where a country road crosses over a brushy ravine with large hayfields on both sides—more than a mile from the milo stubble cited above.

"So you shot a limit of birds, half taken from milo, half from pasture," you say. "On any given day throughout the late 1980s and continuing into the early '90s, that describes a lot of hunters' success throughout the eastern half of Kansas. What's the big deal?"

That perspective is at least partly correct. This has been a year of such abundant quail production that harvesting another limit of birds is no rare accomplishment. However, when I got those quail home, spread them out on the mudroom countertop and began dressing, cleaning and packaging them for the host/landowner's skillet, a wildlife nutrition lesson unfolded.

The four quail we shot over milo stubble had crops stuffed full of seed grains and weed seeds; they were plump birds with small strips of excess fat tissue at the base of their necks and breasts. The crops of the four pasture quail we bagged contained fresh green bits of fleshy leaves, and their food tubes indicated they'd been eating the same thing for several days. These leaf-eating birds were very thin, with much smaller flight muscles and legs so lean the remaining muscle tissue was translucent.

A few days later, at the end of a noon-hour racquetball workout with Kevin Church, upland bird biologist at the Emporia-based research offices of Kansas Wildlife and Parks, I described my quail observations. He wasn't especially surprised and even suggested that what I'd observed was typical for birds occupying grain-field versus pasture habitats—especially during this later part of winter.

Church described three things the conservation-conscious quail hunter can do at this point in the season. First, we can limit our hunting to good cover in and around grain fields where there will be an adequate supply of high-energy, high-nutrition foods into early spring.

Second (and this one is tough for us to do in the heated action of great dog work and fine shooting), we can stop pressing coveys whose numbers are reduced to seven or eight quail. As they form their trademark circular roosting positions at night, with tails toward the center of the group and heads pointed away from the circle to maintain more vigilance in all directions, they are also benefiting from the group's radiated body heat. When their numbers dwindle below about eight birds, a covey is more vulnerable to predators and to loss of optimum shared body heat.

A third proactive step (and even tougher to do when we're having a marginal quail day afield): We hunters can stop hunting at or before 4:30 p.m., thereby giving the birds ample daylight to snuggle back together before nightfall.

Look at it from the game bird's perspective. When we and our dogs push and scatter a covey right down to flat-slap sunset, the birds are challenged to spend a dusky twilight hour or more trying to regroup— at the very same slice of time when (a) Mother Nature's varsity team of daytime quail predators (several hawk species come to mind) are just wrapping up their normal shift and (b) an overlapping all-star cast of nighttime stalkers (owls, feral farm cats, foxes, skunks, bobcats) are bringing their empty stomachs to the fray.

Lots of interactive variables influence the health of any given upland game-bird population. But if the ethical, conservation-minded quail hunters we choose to hunt with can follow the guidelines Church suggests, these simple conservation steps may increase the probability of successful sport hunting for our kids and grandkids.

Chapter 3

Field-Mouse Follies with Ol' Green

January 1996 and 2012

Gazette Editor's Note: Suffering from the frustration of another upland bird-challenged hunting season throughout much of east-central Kansas, our intrepid outdoor columnist has asked us to reprint one of his offerings from the mid-1990s as an attempt to provide hunters a brief escape from what we hope is a temporary skimpy-quail-year depression.

*

We bought the old '71 Chevy step-side pickup from a relative a few years back. Fourteen-year-old son Eric and I rescued it from a tangle of head-high horseweeds behind a slumping wooden barn, and we eagerly designated it project-of-the-year truck, something we would work on together.

With fading Department of Agriculture green-and-gray paint, lots of rust, wrinkles and other signs of aging, the truck definitely needed work. The driver's side door had been pretty badly crumpled at some point in the vehicle's checkered past. But no matter how blemished the truck was, both of us could see the hidden potential even before we towed it out of the weeds and home. What's that line from Tom T. Hall? "I love little baby ducks, old pickup trucks, and slow movin' trains."

Grandpa towed us home behind his newer '72 Chevy, dusty but happy, with our truck's carburetor and air cleaner bouncing on the bench-style seat between us. An old sock had been stuffed in the engine where the carburetor used to be, probably to keep the field mice and pack rats out of the intake manifold. And there were two or three spare tires and rusty wheels in the wood-lined bed.

For the next several months, Eric and I filled spare moments and an occasional Saturday puttering with Ol' Green. The engine block may have been the only part of our project that didn't have a mouse nest in it. During the two years the truck had been sitting in the tall weeds behind that Flint Hills barn, the original seat and glove box had acquired so much "essence of field mouse" that they simply had to be replaced. So much of the material with which they were fabricated was saturated with mouse droppings and urine that our nostrils were burning and our eyes watering. No amount of scrubbing and spraying with Lysol could remove or disguise the aroma.

During our shared project, we discovered a whole new realm of therapy. Nothing erases the day-to-day stresses of the world quite like crawling around in the weeds and the dust of an auto salvage yard, removing parts from scrapped pickup trucks, taking scavenged parts home, and cleaning and recycling them through another old pickup.

The day we got enough pieces back in place so that we could try to start the engine was particularly memorable. While I turned the ignition key, Eric, sitting on top of the radiator, leaned under the hood and held a spark-plug wire a fraction of an inch from its designated spark plug to see if we were getting any fire.

We were.

With a garbled sputter, the old six-cylinder came to life. After the smoking and wheezing subsided, Eric picked himself off the ground, brushed off his jeans, and rubbed his singed eyebrows. His excited grin, nicely accented with just a smudge of grease on one cheekbone, will remain forever in my memory. "Ol' Green's runnin', Dad! Let's drive it up to Grandpa's. He won't believe it!"

Five minutes later and one mile up the hill, we were parked in Grandpa's circle drive with the parking brake set, the gear shift in neutral, the hood raised, and all three of us standing at the front fenders, peering in and listening to that old straight-six engine—humming more quietly than anyone but shade-tree mechanics might have dreamed. Grandpa's farmer's-hand squeeze of Eric's shoulder and a wink toward both of us were all the affirmation this project needed.

Through the next year, we used that old pickup to drive to and from the hayfield; to tow a wood splitter to neighboring timber to cut, split and haul firewood home; to visit creek pools and fishing ponds near and far; to hunt with a kennel of four Brittanys that took turns riding in a new, two-dog box fashioned to fit the truck's vintage bed—all kinds of country chores. Gradually we completed enough brake and engine work and added wheels and tires that were sufficiently sporty for Eric to be willing to drive Ol' Green to school once he got that prized learner's to-and-from permit.

Vehicles have come and gone around our place, but Ol' Green was a near-permanent member of the family. And through it all, whenever we drove the truck far enough for the engine to get really warm, particularly if we had the windows rolled up to ward off the chill, there was still that lingering hint of "essence of field mouse"—that is, until early one weekday afternoon in December.

I'd gotten home from a meeting that was refreshingly short, with a couple of unexpected bonus hours before sundown. So what better way to spend them than with Parker, the Brittany in our kennel that had enjoyed less field work that bird season than any of the other dogs? I loaded this strong-willed, thick-bodied 4-year-old in the dog box in the back of Ol' Green, slid an ancient Remington pump gun and shot-shell vest across the seat, and went rattling down the gravel road toward a half section of what I hoped was still quail-infested creek-bottom milo stubble.

There were so many holes in the rusted floor of the truck that two minutes out of our driveway, the chilly draft prompted me to reach over and push the heater and blower levers to their full-blast position.

Well, the knob on the heater lever broke off in my hand. But at least the heat switch was on. We could jimmy the switch to the off position with needle-nose pliers next spring, right?

The first thing that came out of one of the floor-level openings of the heater vent was a live mouse. And he/she/it seemed to be in a hurry. Even if a mouse running around underfoot as you drive along doesn't particularly frighten you, the animal does get your attention. So I was already looking down when the next thing the heater belched was a small, pungent cloud of dense gray smoke, followed quickly by a couple of wads of mouse-nest material that burst into flame! I think it was about this time when the significance of the broken heater-switch control began to sink in.

Just before the interior of the cab became completely engulfed in choking smoke, I managed to get the driver's-side window rolled down and then the passenger-side window. By this time, I'm pretty sure I'd driven for some distance first in one roadside ditch and then the other.

Somehow I managed to stomp out the flaming mouse-nest material, but the heater was pumping suffocating smoke into Ol' Green faster than it could escape through all available openings. With my head hanging out of the driver's-side window while a panic-stricken Parker barked from inside the dog box, I pulled into Grandpa's driveway, hoping to steer within reach of his garden hose without setting his house on fire.

Then an amazing thing happened: When I came to a stop and shut off the ignition key, off went the engine and heater fan, out went the fire, and within a minute or two, most of the smoke subsided.

For weeks after, the heater would still burp an occasional puff of smoking nest material. And throughout Parker's hour in the field that day, he gave me a disdainful snort every time his path crossed downwind from me and my fragrant clothing. But, other than these minor distractions, things have teetered back to normal around our place. Normal, that is, except for the challenge of trying to find somebody in a rapidly shrinking network of friends and extended family who is willing to drive (or ride in) a 1971 Chevy step-side pickup that used to emit just a faint "essence of field mouse" but now saturates every square centimeter of your clothing with the pungency of smoldering mouse nest!

Hmm. Maybe if we leave it sitting out behind Grandpa Buffon's barn all winter with the windows rolled down ... Naah! It'd just attract more field mice.

Chapter 4

On the Importance of Not Always Bagging Our Limit

January 2011

Today's milder winter temperatures bring to mind an upland bird hunt on an unseasonably warm Saturday in late January back in the 1980s.

The angle of a late-afternoon sun produced long shadows in front of our station wagon as it rolled homeward on Highway 36 along the tier of counties capping north-central Kansas. Seven tired bird hunters plus all our gear rode home in a two-vehicle convoy headed back to Emporia at the end of a long day of walking the rolling fields of Republic County.

There was ample drive time and motivation to wrestle with answers to a question generations of hunters have wrestled with: How might the quality of a hunt be measured by something other than the number of birds we carry home in our game bag?

The question might have been a comfort in other times, including a few near-birdless dove and quail hunts of recent years. But on this day, none of us really needed that much sympathy. As the miles toward home rolled by, an imaginary interview concerning the day's events played out in my head, unfolding something like this:

Opening volley of questions: "How," you ask, "could seven bird hunters ...

- Roust themselves from warm beds in the wee hours of a January night;

- Meet at and depart from a friend's Chase County farm at 4:45 a.m.;

- Drive northwest for four hours to the host farm near Cuba, Kansas;

- Get the host farmer's helpful suggestions for which fields to focus on;

- Hunt hard, marching five or six abreast with one and sometimes two hunters "blocking" at the end of each passage, crossing through milo stubble and brushy draws that seemed to have been reserved for hen pheasants only;

- Break for lunch in a tiny town near the Nebraska border that most of us had never heard of;

- Spend an almost birdless afternoon the most memorable feathered feature of which was flushing a big covey of quail that disappeared over the top of a steep, grassy knoll, cresting that rise in hot pursuit, and watching slack-jawed as that beautiful covey settled to earth near the fenced edge of a little country cemetery—at the very moment a small funeral procession of cars and pickup trucks was entering the front roadside gate for a burial service;

- Retreat to our host family's farmhouse for thanks all around and depart for home near sunset, stiff and leg-weary, arrive home well after dark, with a grand total of two pheasants ... and still feel good about the trip?"

My answer: "Well, it may be difficult to explain—and even harder for some folks to understand. Did you by chance read last week's column? I, er, uh, tried to address this issue."

Next question: "Who were the members of this hunting party?"

Answer: "Well, let's see. There was Morris Eidman, his son Steve and Mo's brother Gene from rural Chase County; their longtime friend, Carl Garrison from Coffeyville, and Francis Morgan and his son Mike; plus me, from Emporia.

Q: "Was anybody upset about the meager harvest?"

A: "Not really."

Q: "Did everybody get a shot at a rooster pheasant?"

A: "Well, uh, yes. I think all seven of us got at least one shot at a cock bird."

Next (logical) question: "Does that mean if every hunter in your party had hit the pheasant(s) he shot at, your group would have brought home at least seven pheasants?"

A: I doubt it. You see, on several occasions two or more of us were probably shooting at the same bird as it flushed out in front of (or behind) us. That happens quite a lot in pheasant hunting, you know … so does shooting behind, below or above our flying target."

Q: "Did you use bird dogs on your hunt?"

A: (Grimace!) "No."

Q: "Doesn't anyone in your party own a bird dog?"

A: "Uh, at least three of us own trained bird dogs. But, well, uh, there was some serious miscommunication among us the night before the hunt and … (whimper)."

Q: "Would a good dog have helped?"

A: "Yes! And here's the day's first reminder: A gaudy pheasant rooster flushed directly in front of Morris and me with that nerve-wracking cackle just as we approached the end of the first crossing of the first field of the day. Mo and I fired, and the bird folded in midair. Having no dog, I sprinted to the spot where the bird fell only to discover he, too, had apparently hit the ground running. After several minutes of searching in the grassy cover at the field's edge, all seven of us spotted a big, lean German shorthair male working back and forth in front of a separate hunting party that was walking a field across the road. The shorthair came out to the road ditch between our respective fields and did what well-trained dogs do: He assumed a 'birdy' posture, crept forward at the road's edge, froze briefly in a classic point, and then pounced on 'our' bird. The dog retrieved the pheasant to the nearest hunter in the other field. We watched dumbfounded as the man patted the dog, held the bird up high in admiration, stuffed it in his hunting vest, and the whole group resumed walking the field without a word—in spite of the fact that not one of them had fired a shot!"

Q: (Sigh) "If a dog might have been helpful, why didn't you take one?"

A: (Bigger sigh) "I can't offer a sensible answer. Several of us have asked ourselves and each other that same question countless times since last Saturday. Our best guess is that each of us dog owners must have thought the other two were bringing their dogs."

Q: "Well, if you brought home just two pheasants, what made this a good hunt?"

A: (After a few seconds' pause and the hint of a smile on my face) "How long has it been since you spent a full day with six friends whose company you genuinely enjoy, exercising your legs with lots of walking, exercising your lungs and diaphragm (and your soul) with periodic bursts of convulsive laughter—about all manner of things—and exercising your pallet and stomach with larrupin'-good cheeseburgers and onion rings in a country town so small you drove the two blocks of Main Street three times and still had to get out of the station wagon, cross the street to the farmers' co-op, and ask a guy pumping diesel fuel into a flatbed Ford to tell you which unmarked building was the café!

"And we did all that on a day that was so sunny and mild it seemed like October."

Last question: "Are you suggesting that even if you knew in advance your party of seven would spend a day like that and come home with just two cock pheasants, you'd still make the trip?"

Last answer: "Every time we get the chance. *Every* time ... but we would bring along at least two seasoned bird dogs."

Chapter 5

Upland Season of Misfortune Finishes Well

February 1986

Could it be that I'm the only hunter in the Flint Hills who found the previous year's upland bird season to be the strangest on record? Come to think of it, the past three seasons didn't provide much local upland gunning to write home about—unless you have a preference for comic tragedies.

In times like these, perhaps we can console ourselves by reflecting on the humorous and the bizarre.

Surely we'd all agree we were in for a strange upland bird season when:

- On a Wednesday in late October, a couple of weeks before the opening of the prairie chicken, pheasant and quail seasons, you explain to friends Dan and Susan that you must regretfully decline their tempting invitation to join them for next Saturday's KU–K State football game, because you have already invited a faculty colleague and his son to join you for a late-season mourning dove shoot over a prime, 20-acre patch of burned-off wheat stubble on that Saturday;

- On KU–KSU game-day morning, you receive a phone call from the same colleague who, with a touch of embarrassment in his voice, explains he and his son will not be able to make the dove hunt because "some new friends of ours, Dan and Susan, phoned just a couple of hours ago, saying they had two extra tickets to the KU–K-State game and ... er ... uh ... ";

- You regroup and make a few last-minute phone calls, finding that guests at recent dove hunts already have their own KU–KSU plans for the afternoon; so ...

- With your oldest Brittany, Pete, along for company, you arrive at your dove-shooting hot spot just in time to watch the landowner/farmer as he and his gimongous John Deere and triple-wide tandem disc are pulling out of that field onto the adjacent dirt road and away from those prime dove acres—with the only feathered visitors remaining being a flock of crows gorging themselves on earthworms exposed in the freshly tilled soil.

At this point in the upland season, you're still cautiously optimistic until:

- Three hunting buddies from out of state telephone you on consecutive days the week before the November pheasant opener and cancel their long-standing reservations for your annual southwest Kansas "rooster reunion" with lame excuses: one is getting married, one is getting a divorce, and the third is undergoing heart bypass surgery;

- You show up on time, as a favorite quail-hunting partner's voice-mail message specified, "for breakfast at his house on opening day," only to find him and the missus backing out of their driveway to attend an antique auction. It seems they had written the quail season opener on their kitchen calendar (and highlighted it in yellow!) for the following weekend;

- Just you and Parker, your youngest and most promising Brittany, hunt a favorite property all morning and neither of you has seen or pointed game, so you finally take a break to share a dried-out sandwich at midafternoon.

And you can be pretty sure it's a strange upland bird season when:

- About midmorning of your second quirky day afield, you miss both shots fired from your favorite side-by-side quail gun when a covey flies straight away from Bess and Pete's stylish point;

- Not two minutes later, these two oldest, most dependable dogs in your kennel seize the opportunity to chase three antlerless deer that break from a small wood lot and continue westward until both deer and dogs disappear over a gentle hill a half mile west of you. Twenty minutes later, when the dogs return, Bess has a 4-inch-long gash between her shoulder blades that could have been achieved only via high-speed contact with the lowest strand of a barbed-wire fence;

- You return from a much-anticipated pheasant hunt in north-central Kansas knowing the square root of the number of cottontail rabbits you and your party stepped on is still twice the number of rooster pheasants seen by anyone, dogs included, from any distance, and therefore the highlight of that trip was the world-class cheeseburger and onion rings you ate at the unmarked (and only) café in Narka, Kansas.

But you can be rock-solid sure it's been a weird bird season when:

- Midway through your next-to-last hunt of the season, you interrupt a month of spouse-promoted conversion to lovable house pet for Kate, the Brittany whose performance has been unpredictable and flaky for most of her three and a half years, offering her one final, nothing-to-lose chance for redemption, whereupon she suddenly starts scenting multiple coveys of quail, pointing, retrieving and generally acting like the seasoned professional her pedigree predicted;

- When you, your father-in-law, your brother-in-law and your dogs find almost as many quail coveys on January 31, the last day of the season, as you did the whole month of December! And you do it in shirtsleeve weather.

Oh well, it may have been a weird season, but upland bird hunters tend to be incurable optimists, right? So how many years has it been since you were even out there chasing them on the last day—harvesting a few and leaving encouraging numbers for future years' gene pool?

Chapter 6

The Real Secret to Outdoor Joy

March 2010

[Originally published in 1988 on the editorial page of The Emporia Gazette under the pen name Masche Field.]

If you've ever known a longtime smoker who's finally kicked the habit, this person may have explained to you that it isn't cigarettes per se that make quitting so difficult; it's all those pleasant sensations and experiences that are almost subconsciously linked to smoking. Has any of us ever heard a tobacco addict suggest this addiction is easy to overcome?

After all, veteran strugglers with nicotine tell us a good smoke goes hand in glove with that first steaming cup of morning coffee; the midmorning cup that helps wash down a whole-wheat cinnamon roll from a favorite mom-and-pop café; the ice-cold beer at sundown with farm friends that washes away the dust and fatigue from stuffing heavy square bales of alfalfa away in the pole barn; the dessert and coffee after a big Sunday dinner with family, and yes, folks, especially after great sex.

Is it any wonder then that in spite of the overwhelming evidence against tobacco consumption, so many people are still hooked?

As a civilization, we are fortunate that no other human habits become psychologically entangled with gratifying experiences, right?

Wrong.

As fate or fortune would have it, most outdoor sporting pursuits (hunting, fishing, camping, hiking, bird-watching) are also hopelessly linked with an almost endless assortment of other gratifying human experiences. If you're absolutely sure you want to save a friend or a loved one from addiction to one of these gloriously healthy outdoor habits, might it follow then that you begin by identifying this person's menu of subconscious reinforcers and somehow help the addict disassociate each one from the joys of hunting quail or catching bass?

I've kept silent on this subject for too long. My conscience compels me to bare the naked truth.

Perhaps I can illustrate by personal example. Even as a youngster (note that this imprinting may begin in early childhood!), I wasn't so much enjoying catching all those sunfish, bullheads, frogs and turtles along a half mile stretch of Dry Creek, where it brushes the northwest corner of Neosho Rapids, Kansas, as I was looking forward to the aroma, the golden-brown crunchy texture, and the heavenly flavor of Mom Irwin's fried chicken, mashed potatoes and gravy and those melt-in-your-mouth hot rolls that followed (reinforced) my mornings along the creek.

During my college years, it wasn't really those weekend retreats for fall bird hunting or spring fishing at the farm of my sister, Myra Lee Love, that I was enjoying; it was Myra's extra-thick hamburgers, made from home-grown beef, served on buns grilled in butter, to say nothing of her homemade cookies and always-fresh coffee or iced tea.

And who says I was growing, learning, honing my outdoor skills and enjoying the friendship of the Dale and Betty Hogan family during visits to Neosho Rapids for weekend retreats during my early years of science teaching? Anyone there could tell you I was really just licking my chops over the meals Betty prepared. Who among us could stop haunting the fields and streams of east Lyon and northwest Coffey counties when we knew we were coming home to Betty's spaghetti and meatballs or her chili soup or her creamed potatoes, complemented with a taste bud–numbing variety of home-grown garden vegetables and topped off with a huge, thick wedge of her butterscotch pie that would make Duncan Hines and Julia Childs stand upright, beat their chests and howl at the moon?

I can't forget all those late-September camping trips to the scenic foothills of the Davis Mountains during my West Texas years. Whether attending an arts-and-crafts fair in the remote hamlet of Fort Davis, roaming the old fort itself, or shooting doves in the nearby irrigated grain fields, I wasn't really enjoying myself all that much; I was merely burning up the calories packed in Gayleen Ienatsch's state-park-campground oatmeal pancakes. Or I was just whetting my appetite for her husband Pete's rib-eye steaks, braised with garlic butter and cooked slowly over a mesquite-fired campground grill at sunset.

And finally, in more recent years, back home in these Flint Hills of Kansas, surely I haven't gained that much satisfaction from joining friends and family as I caught a stringer full of crappies or watched with wonder as a young Brittany pup locked on point downwind from a covey of quail. I was only filling the hours between those mouth-watering meals served in rural Chase County at Professor Sophie Thayer's table or at Morris and Mary Jo Eidman's home or waiting for the chicken and the homemade noodles at the fall harvest supper hosted by the Saffordville UMC ladies at the old Toledo Township High School building.

One word of caution: If you choose to try some kind of amateurish, harebrained scheme to help yourself, your friends or your loved ones to disassociate perfectly healthy (some say therapeutic!) outdoor sporting pursuits involving equally gratifying, life-changing relationships from culinary reinforcers such as those listed above, this writer and the publisher of this newspaper will not be responsible for any sudden increase in attempted suicides among the ranks of our heretofore well-adjusted, rock-solid readers.

However, if you do decide to try such amateur therapy, it might be a good idea to check the last entry in the appendix at the back of this book for the recipe for the apple cake regularly served through many seasons by a legendary one-room-country-school teacher, the late Marguerite "Granny" Buffon. Whether your foray into improving mental health is successful or not, you'll need the reinforcement.

Chapter 7

Wrap Up Hunting; Pond Fish're Biting!

February 2012

There we were, navigating the maze that is a downtown Kansas City parking garage three levels below last Saturday's PheasantFest, hosted by the upland bird conservation twins Pheasants Forever/Quail Forever in Bartle Hall convention center, when a cell phone chirped. Neighbor, outdoor friend, fly fisherman and driver for today's excursion Bill Hartman said, "I think that's your cell."

After 10 seconds of that all-too-familiar awkward groping to retrieve a phone sandwiched somewhere under my seat belt, the voice of a farmer/stockman/friend Gene Eidman came through with crystal clarity from the shoreline of one of his Chase County Flint Hills pasture ponds: "If you're still accepting outdoor reports from the field, I thought you'd want to know those crappie and bass you were catching during those warm days of last week are flirtin' with us again."

Gene paused long enough to get my "Glad to hear it" and then added, "My friend Andy drove out our way this afternoon to try the rod-and-reel remedy for a touch of spring fever. When we got over to the southeast pond, I handed him one of those H&H spinner lures you gave me. He tied it on and in no time hooked a nice big ol' crappie!"

Gene went on to say that neighbor youngsters had been fishing his ponds for crappie and bass with good success on some of the warm afternoons of recent weekends—using spinning lures.

Then, two days ago, fishing the downwind shoreline of three ponds in western Lyon and eastern Chase counties, my German shorthair Shani and I enjoyed some fleeting (10- to 30-minute) bass and crappie feeding sprees. Black-and-white-skirted and chartreuse-and-white-skirted H&H single-spin lures were catching the crappie on every second or third cast for a brief span.

And just today, news via the cell phone network included a report that Gene's brother, Morris Eidman, while fishing "a nice clear-water pond somewhere in the three-county span between Marion and Emporia," caught some healthy late-winter crappie in the 12- to 15-inch range using soft wiggle-tail Swimmin' Minnow lures on a one-eighth-ounce jig head.

Indeed, we're entering the season of sweeping swings of air temperature and pressure and the raw, blustery winds they produce; but the second afternoon of any two-day sequence of sunshine and 50-plus degrees offers you a better-than-even chance of hooking something edible from the downwind shallows of your favorite clear-water farm pond or watershed impoundment.

Get out of the house and enjoy!

Late-winter farm-pond bass meets silver
blade No. 3 Mepps Streamer lure!

*Early-spring crappies respond to a variety of
spinning lures including this black Beetle.*

Part Two: Spring Overview

What is it about those first few outings of spring? Is it the eagerness of anglers of all ages to shake off winter and wet a hook and line? Is it the relative ease with which we catch those spring farm-pond bass and crappie after a few consecutive days of warmer temperatures? Is it the energy we're willing to spend in tackling house, lawn and garden chores if only to ease our priority consciousness as we plot and engineer the next round of spring-fever hooky?

Is it that magic weekend in April when the leaves of Osage orange trees reach the size of squirrels' ears—the Old Farmer's Almanac signal that the bass and pan fish will start smacking those popping bugs and Hula Poppers any day now?

Is it the bittersweet memories generated by Memorial Day—preferably shared with family and close friends?

A decent return on a 40-minute investment at
Pickett's "old pond," Lyon County, Kansas.

Chapter 8

Does Fishing with a Boy Trump Searching for One?

March 1988

Every fish in that stretch of the creek must have known we were there, standing on the downstream tip of a tiny gravel bar. We hadn't been particularly quiet as we stepped out of the pickup and over the fence with our rods and pocket packs of spinners and slid down the bank and onto the familiar gravel.

Eric watched closely as I tied a quarter-ounce brownish orange, crawdad-colored H&H spinner lure on his line. He remembered to check for any overhanging vegetation behind him, crooked his arm and flexed his wrist into the first cast.

Even though his seventh birthday is still two months away, the little guy is already showing some skill with that Crappie Spin rod-and-reel combo, I thought to myself as he placed the lure just inches away from prop roots at the base of a slender elm growing out of the opposite shoreline. "Kerploop!"

Two cranks of the reel handle and the light rod was bending and dancing. The boy squealed with delight as he stopped reeling and shuffle-walked backward along the gravel bar until he'd dragged a wiggly, flopping 1-pound bass to higher ground. He lipped the fish with thumb and forefinger like

Grandpa Morris had taught him and held it up for eye-level examination in the Chase County sunshine.

"The hook is really stuck in the top of his mouth, Dad. Could you help me get him loose?" he asked. In the time it took Dad to unhook the fish, turn around to place it in our wire live basket and tie the basket's cord to a willow limb, the boy had hooked another one.

Half an hour later, we were driving away from the creek around the edge of soybean stubble and alfalfa. Eric was remarkably calm for a 6-year-old who'd just caught and released half a dozen "keeper" creek bass. His dad may have been prouder and more pleased than anyone. Even before we stepped away from the creek, Eric said matter of factly, "This part of the creek is on Granny's farm, Dad. So let's take some fish to her and Grampa."

We drove home with a healthy pair of three-quarter-pound bass, filleted them and packaged them in a quart-size Zip-Loc bag. Then we drove back down the hill, and Eric presented them to Great-Grandpa and Grandma Buffon, who later assured the boy that they were the best-tasting fish they'd ever eaten.

Everything in this account is just as my youngest son and I enjoyed it—late one golden afternoon early last October.

*

We know there are other important things going on this Easter weekend. But late Sunday afternoon, well after the morning service, the extended family picnic and the final egg hunt, one small boy and his dad will feel the need to make sure the bass and the sunfish in a clear, quiet pool below a tiny gravel bar on Granny B's branch of Buckeye Creek made it through the winter in good health.

Who knows? It just might tell us something about our own condition.

We have some beautiful spring weekends ahead of us. With apologies to the folks who wrote the popular jingle for one of AT&T's [1980s–'90s] long-distance telephone commercials, we'd like to offer a slight variation that seems to fit: "Reach out*doors* and touch someone you love."

Chapter 9

Spring Fishing in Farm Ponds—Just Do It!

March 1990

All right! Here's the scene: You've had a bellyful of winter, a spring (so far) full of more winter, and you've read all available outdoor-magazine articles and newspaper columns about fishing. It's time to do it.

You can take down the storm windows and hang the screens next week. We're burnin' sunlight here. And you can clean out and reorganize the garage on the next cold, rainy day. It's time to go fishing!

Keep things simple. Grab a rod and reel, a few basic lures or baits, a stringer or wire live basket, and head for your favorite farm pond.

Why a farm pond? Because. Catching fish in a farm pond is simple—unless you and/or the weather make it complicated. The water in ponds is shallower than in large impoundments. Therefore it warms more quickly as spring approaches. A few consecutive days of sunshine, and crappie and bass move into the shallows, sometimes just a few feet offshore.

If there's a breeze, concentrate on the downwind shoreline—at least in early spring. Wind pushes the waves to one side of the pond. The wave action mixes more oxygen and warmth into the water on the downwind side. Fish, and all the smaller critters in their food web, gravitate toward the warmer, more oxygenated water.

Farm-pond fishing doesn't require fancy tackle. Tie on a No. 2 or 3 Mepps spinner with a squirrel-tail dressing on the treble hook, or a quarter- or three-eighths-ounce Beetle Spin in almost any color. Cast and retrieve, cast and retrieve, cast and retrieve. Stand in a likely spot and cast into the shallows adjacent or parallel to the shore or surface vegetation—to your left and right. If you don't get a strike in 10 to 12 casts, move down the shoreline and repeat the pattern.

If the pond you've chosen has fish, you're gonna catch something. If you don't, move to another pond and try all over again.

The worst thing that can happen is you might have to spend part of a beautiful day outdoors and come home with no fish to clean.

Yep, the NIKE sporting goods folks got it right: "Just Do It!"

Chapter 10

Spring's First Family Bass Bash

April 1984

We looked longingly at the surface of the pond—the way you do when you haven't visited the same body of water since this time last spring. In spite of all the recent thunderstorms, the water was surprisingly clear, with just a hint of a ripple from a gentle southwest breeze. When you've walked half a mile from the nearest road, loaded down with rod, reel and a tackle box with six times more lures than your entire party of four could use and lose in a week, it's reassuring to find the water clear and inviting—bassy lookin' water.

The modest hike from the car paid off immediately for son Chris. His second cast with a black-and-white-skirted H&H single spin produced a scrappy largemouth bass, a pound-and-a-half eatin'-size keeper.

Nephew Stan and my son Matt quickly followed with strikes of their own. Finally, even ol' Dad joined the fray with a solid hit on his green shad-colored Pico Perch plug, and we were off to the races. What followed was almost a classic, textbook morning in grassland pond fishing.

What is it about that first outing of the spring for bass or crappie that's so special? Several things made this one stand out.

It was the first serious bass fishing my sons, my nephew and I had been able to schedule following a long, gray winter. To be sure, we wanted to start the day with a good pond, a known producer, one where we'd caught fish in previous years and where the landowner would make us feel welcome. This first pond met all those criteria. But with all the recent rainfall, there was always a chance that the water might be a little turbid.

Under the best conditions, largemouth bass can be tough to locate and to trick into striking at a funny-looking, jangling piece of hardware. But because most of the sunfish family are sight feeders, when the water is murky or downright muddy, the fish cannot see your lure as clearly. So the odds are stacked against you. Hence the quiet relief we felt when we'd crossed the last fence and walked up to the edge of clear, grass-filtered water.

This trip was also special because, for the four of us, it was one of those days when we just happened to be in the right place at the right time and doing the right things to catch fish! We'd enjoyed very few days more than this one. Practically everything we threw caught bass; H&H spinners caught fish; Scorpion and Tarantula spinners caught fish; Pico Perch and Storm King plugs (in several color patterns and sizes) caught fish; Mepps spinners caught bass (but when haven't they?); even a large black Jitterbug caught a fish—a little bass not much bigger than the plug itself. Everything caught fish!

The day's gratification was enhanced because my sons and my nephew shared it.

After little more than an hour of catching and releasing dozens of scrappy bass and putting maybe a half-dozen keepers in the live basket, the action tapered off almost as quickly as it began. It was as if the fishes' feeding period was timed to say to us, "Very well, gentlemen. You've had your fun. But fair's fair. You've harvested enough from this small ecosystem. Move on. Go home and grace the dining table with your share of our surplus, but take no more for now."

So we left that small, blue jewel in the Flint Hills, but not without a new chapter of memories—till the next time out—or perhaps that first special outing of a distant spring.

A dozen different lures, including H&H reflex single spinners, caught fish in this pond.

Chapter 11

Sharing the Catch Is Still Special

April 2012

The pond was very small but the water was clear, as it usually is in midspring. Jeb had made no more than four or five casts with an ultralight outfit when he felt that delicate telltale bump and quick dance of the short rod tip that said, "Crappie on!"

The first one of the day still produces a special feeling. Even though this shimmering, silvery, wiggling specimen with the dark spots on its sides was no thicker and not much larger than Jeb's hand, an idea formed and he slipped this first fish of the day into a woven wire live basket.

Two casts later the tiny white Beetle Spin nailed another. Then a black bass of less than a pound impaled herself on the same lure; soon another.

Jeb placed all four and a dozen more in his wire live basket in the next half hour—but not with the idea of keeping them for his skillet. Less than a half mile away, across a gravel road and up another grassy pasture slope, lay a larger, deeper pond, nestled in a deep cut in the hillside.

Ten or more years ago this larger pond produced some impressive stringers of bass and crappie. But in all Jeb's return trips through the intervening years, he'd managed just a single early-March bass of about 3 pounds, and not so much as another strike.

So after the sun hid behind a cloud bank and the short feeding run ended, Jeb lifted the basket, admired this first catch of spring, and hustled the fish off to the big pond across the road—as breeding stock for the future.

While Jeb was releasing the fish, a second thought formed and he kept one back—a beautiful, skillet-size bass of about one-and-a-quarter pounds that yielded two beautiful, boneless fillets that brought a broad smile to the warm, round face of the landowner widow.

As we drove down the country road toward home, it occurred to me that Jeb's first fishing trip of the spring had turned out well from just about every angle. (Oops!)

First, my friend caught those fish from a pond neither of us had fished before and didn't know much about or have much expectation for—just because he took the time and extended the respect and the courtesy to ask the landlady's permission.

Second, Jeb caught those fish from a pond that the landowner herself wasn't all that optimistic about. She was at least as pleasantly surprised as we were when he handed her the plastic bag of fillets.

Third, it was possible to do a little restocking of the bigger pond nearby, an old favorite, with the hope of providing a small investment for future fishing. If you're familiar with the reproductive potential of bass and crappie, you know that those few hand-size specimens my friend took from the smaller pond and transplanted to the larger one probably improved the growth opportunities for both fisheries.

Finally, the pleasure two nice bass fillets gave the gentle lady who took a chance and let a couple of strangers fish in one of her ponds is our idea of a good return on a modest investment—good for everyone involved.

Chapter 12

Some Lures Do Catch
Muddy-Water Bass

May 1987

Jett stepped up to a favorite bass pond a day or two after a heavy local thunderstorm, took one look at the water's muddy texture and nearly walked away.

You may have read some of those publications that school us on how bass are primarily sight feeders, thereby making muddy water a poor place to try to convince such top-of-the-food-pyramid predators that any artificial lure you're dangling before them looks like something they eat on a regular basis.

Tain't necessarily so. And last Friday evening Jett's instincts nudged him to suspend judgment about that pond full of clouded water long enough to try a few casts.

Early that day he had phoned a farmer in the Olpe area whose ponds he hadn't fished for a couple of years. They had usually been productive enough; Jett had just turned his life and his fishing attention elsewhere and had temporarily forgotten about them.

The farmer's wife answered his call, remembered him and said, "We've had to padlock all the pasture gates for the last couple of years, Jett. Some people got to taking advantage of us and nearly had a paved road worn between the boundary road and the biggest pond. So we locked 'em up."

There was a little pause, but then she said, "You can go ahead and try your luck, Jett, if you'll park by the gate on the south side of that section, crawl under the fence, and walk in to the ponds. But don't expect much. My husband and I used to enjoy those ponds regularly, but they've gotten so mossy in recent years they're difficult to fish. And the bigger pond is pretty murky most of the time. We don't know why; it never used to be."

They visited a while longer, and then Jett thanked her and promised to let her know if he had any luck.

An hour later, he parked his battered little Dodge pickup on the south border of that grassy section, strapped on his small belly box of lures, and a five-minute hike later, he was standing on the shore of a large farm pond whose water was the color of coffee with extra cream. Much of the pond's perimeter was covered with a thick, floating mass of algae extending out from shore as much as 15 feet in places.

Jett studied that water for a minute as his mind wandered back a few years to visits he'd made there during which he'd caught some hefty bass in crystal-clear water. What had changed? He looked around and couldn't see anything so different. The pond still drained onto nothing but gentle slopes covered with native grasses. Sure, the pasture had been part of the "every third spring burn," but that had been more than a month earlier. And yes, cattle were scattered in a far quarter of the pasture, but there'd been cattle cooling themselves and drinking from the ponds in that pasture every summer he could remember.

So, for better or worse, there he was, looking at a pond that certainly fit the owner's description—and was less than encouraging.

During his high school years, Jett had been a slashing, top-notch linebacker and wrestler and had earned a "never quit" reputation. Poking around among the small collection of lures in his belly box, he came up with a brown-skirted Strike King with a big, single spinner blade—the kind that vibrates your rod tip as you retrieve it. He reasoned if the water was too muddy for the bass to see the lure, maybe they'd feel those vibrations.

On the second or third cast, just at the edge of and parallel to that mossy apron of algae, the surface of the water exploded as the strike of a well-hooked 3-pounder blasted the brown plastic skirt trailing that spinner. Two casts later, as Jett reeled that throbbing lure closer toward shore, and with only 3 or 4 feet of line extending from his rod tip, he started to lift the lure out over the floating apron of algae and *wham!* An apparent clone of the first bass smashed the lure.

Minutes later, Jett had caught and released two more bass—one scaled 3½ pounds and the last an even 4.

A few evenings later and just two days after another thunderstorm, Jett invited me to fish two ponds in the pasture of a mutual friend. These ponds, normally very clear, were also quite cloudy with the last storm's run-off. So, following my young friend's grinning account of his earlier murky-water triumph, I tied on a black-skirted Strike King with that big, vibrating spinner blade. In the next half hour, we caught and released a dozen bass of 1 pound or more.

The landowner insisted the pond was overpopulated and urged us to keep some. So we brought home three, filleted them, and tried a fly-fishing neighbor's favorite recipe. We whipped equal amounts of egg and mustard into a batter, dipped the fish strips into the batter, dredged them in roller-pinned crumbs of Triscuit crackers, fried the fillets in olive oil to light brown, drained the fish on paper towels, and served it with baked potato and a chilled fruit salad. Our only regret was that we didn't bring home two more bass and invite both farmers and their wives to join us!

There seems to be a lesson in this: before we give up on fishing for bass in muddy water, we'd do well to tie on a large spinner, cast and retrieve with enough vigor to feel the rod tip vibrating, and get a good grip on the rod handle!

A few nights later, Jett reported, "It was just pure enjoyable to phone the owners of both farms and assure them their ponds may look mossy and murky occasionally, but they sure aren't dead."

Chapter 13

Wade-Fishing a Flint Hills Creek: Pure Therapy

May 1993

How long has it been since you took a Huck Finn kind of day, escaped from the cares of the world and dipped a toe or dangled a worm on a hook in the shaded waters of a favorite creek?

Enjoying a break from university teaching between spring term and summer school, last Tuesday I interrupted several days of yard work around our home in the Flint Hills to wade a couple of miles of quiet pools and gentle riffles along the west branch of Buckeye Creek in northeast Chase County.

Preparations began in the long shadows of the evening before this adventure. I phoned ahead and then drove over to the neighboring Glendale Ranch to confirm access arrangements with foreman Joe Henry. As I drove in the gravel lot next to an elongated white barn and a machine shed, Joe was finishing after-supper chores with a nice string of beagles who greeted my arrival with a melodious chorus from within a well-designed kennel shaded by a pair of ancient cottonwood trees.

With a slight jerk of his head toward the pens and in that deep, south Georgia voice, Joe said, "When the wintah winds are slantin' just right out uh the northwest, I reckon y'all

can hea-uh these crittahs a howlin' from clear over ta yo-ah place"—
to which I replied, "Yes sir, and proud of it! On some of those frosty
November mornings and evenings when I'm tending to the Brittanys in
our kennel, it seems you must be doin' the same. It's great sound comin'
across the land from your branch of the creek to ours."

Before I could restate my telephone request from 20 minutes before,
Joe summarized, "Now, y'all are wantin' to leave yer old wrinkled
pickup jus' down the hill from the house and around that bend by the
crick crossing?" As I was nodding with a grateful smile, he glanced at
his watch and said, "I'm s'posed ta meet a fella in half an hour about
renewin' one of our grazin' leases ovuh by Strong City. So drive yer truck
down to tomorrow's take-out point; I'll follah, pick y'all up and carry ya
home on my way to Strong."

The next morning as the sound of the six o'clock news, sports and
weather on the garage radio diminished, I walked the quarter-mile
length of our driveway and a mile southwest from our home, across the
east branch of Buckeye Creek, and another half mile on to a low-water
bridge on the west branch, which put me some two miles downstream
from my eventual Glendale Ranch take-out point. I was armed with
nothing more than a lightweight spinning rod and two shirt pockets
full of one-eighth-ounce lures.

Working slowly and quietly up the creek from a gentle riffle above the
low-water bridge, I waded from pool to pool, casting several different
lures. Eventually, I settled on a 2-inch, black-and-white soft-plastic
wiggly-tail bait threaded on a one-eighth-ounce lead-head jig. Of the
limited supply of lures I was carrying, that one looked most like the
minnows that fanned out ahead of me as I eased my way through pools
of shining water.

From time to time throughout the morning, I'd add a tiny reflex spinner
to the jig with fair success. The first customer was a 10-inch black bass,
followed by a thick-bodied bluegill. I admired both in the shaded
morning light and then released them, allowing them to get on with
their day.

Good numbers of gray-green crayfish scurrying ahead of my old canvas high-top tennis shoes prompted me to switch to a lure that resembled them (the crawdads, not the "tennies"), and sure enough, I hooked a scrappy 1-pound spotted bass, a well-known crawdad predator found in a number of Chase County watersheds. But retying the black-and-white minnow jig produced the most consistent results.

Examples shown are one-eighth-ounce lures
proven effective for creek wade fishing.

And good results they were. Although I did not make notes or take photos and had no witnesses, I'm sure I hooked and released 40 to 50 small bass and fat bluegill. The largest fish of the day, a largemouth bass, might have tipped the scales at 2 pounds, but most were smaller, yet scrappy.

From one tiny pool just below a slight riffle, I hooked a glistening, silvery half-pound channel catfish. Two casts later into that same pool, using the same black-and-white minnow with the little spinner added, I hooked and released a fat, golden-yellow bullhead. The feisty little catfish took the lure and lunged downstream with the force of a fish three times its bulk.

Having no timepiece, I was mildly surprised when a wide gap in the trees near a beautiful little waterfall revealed that the sun was almost directly overhead. I looked down at my shadow, quite short and pointing toward what had to be north. This prompted me to climb the east bank of the creek and look across the landscape to check my bearings with known landmarks. An old limestone barn shining in the sun across a deep- green alfalfa field told me I'd traveled only about half the planned course.

The remainder of the day went much the same—beautiful pools stretching before me, most with solid rock or gravel bottoms, interrupted at intervals by shallow riffles where water tumbled over layers of algae-covered limestone. The wading was for the most part quite easy. The water was waist deep in a good many pools though I sank to the armpits at a couple of sharp bends in the stream's meandering course. On several occasions the current and the sudden chill of spring water around my knees indicated underwater seams between layers of limestone injecting steady currents of more life-giving fluid into this beautiful little ecosystem.

As I continued the gentle climb along the watercourse's spillage through the hills, the pools became smaller and shallower. Yet, in a scenic stretch of shaded stream below my take-out point, I caught the most beautiful fish of the day—a silvery, black-spotted crappie that would weigh more than a pound. Just as I released her to waist-deep water, a whitetail buck shattered the silence with that trademark snort and thrashed through streamside ragweed and sting nettle—an animal caught off guard.

I walked up the two-track from the graveled low-water crossing to the old green pickup just in time to turn the ignition key and hear the trusty AM radio piping out the five o'clock news—which explained the empty driveway next to the ranch foreman's house as neither Joe nor his attractive and personable wife, Karin, was home from work yet. So I penciled a short note and wedged it in the screen-door latch, thanking them for allowing me access to the day's therapy.

As I bent to release this last crappie, a magnificent whitetail buck sprang from thick streamside cover—one more bonus feature of a day filled with them.

The slow drive home gave me time to take stock of the day and the resident wildlife I had seen and heard along this Flint Hills watercourse. The list is too long to include in its entirety. In addition to all the fish caught and released, the creek showed off its turtles, frogs, snails, tadpoles and crayfish of various sizes, a muskrat, two beaver, and a raccoon that worked the creek bank not 15 feet opposite me for several minutes before the breeze shifted enough that he caught my scent, gave a start and disappeared beneath the prop roots of an ash tree at water's edge.

Along with the trophy whitetail buck, I spotted two does, many fox squirrels and a coyote far across a creek-side pasture and saw or heard countless birds, observing the timeless skirmish between a great horned owl and a half-dozen crows. There were wild turkeys, quail and all the usual songbirds that contribute to the creek bottom community— woodpeckers, kingfishers, grackles and jays. Bonus sightings included two pheasants near the edge of the alfalfa (a little unusual for this far east in Kansas) and a pair of wood ducks that sprang from a long creek pool above a beaver dam and flew down through the tunnel of overarching trees extending from both banks.

Our kennel of Brittanys performed a recognition dance on their hind legs as the old green pickup eased down the long driveway at home. To be sure, I felt tired from the day's wading and walking. I had eaten only a handful of ripe mulberries at midday from a tree upstream from the waterfall. I had not taken anything to drink. Yet I did not feel undue hunger or thirst.

My cup runneth over.

Guess where a resident pair of belted kingfishers built their nest.

Chapter 14

Thanks, Brother-in-Law

May 1988

Brother-in-law Steve Eidman had been telling us for a week that it was beautiful water. At scattered intervals throughout the hour-long drive into an obscure section of east-central Kansas' Flint Hills, there were additional hints that we were in for a special treat.

As advertised, at day's end, as we drove toward the main ranch gate and headed home with a stringer and a wire fish basket sagging from the weight of crappie and largemouth bass, at least two of us, father-in-law Morris Eidman and I, were still pinching ourselves and expecting to wake up any minute from the ultimate Great Plains angler's dream.

Undoubtedly, events more profoundly important and newsworthy were happening on the afternoon of Wednesday, May 25, 1988. But the three of us who spent that afternoon on a beautiful, clear watershed lake deep in the heart of tallgrass prairie believe we have established a whole new standard by which all future small-water fishing trips will be compared.

Did we catch the largest fish of our lives? No.

Did we catch more fish than at any time in our memories? No, not really.

All we did was spend three to four hours catching crappie and bass with only one brief lull in the action—and we did it with an intriguing variety of baits and lures. We caught crappie on minnows, jigs, horsehead spinner-jigs, spinners and crank baits.

We caught and released bass, including a dozen or more in the 2- to 4-pound range, till our thumbs were raw from removing hooks from their rough-textured mouths. We caught them on Mepps spinners, Beetle Spins, crank baits—especially those resembling crawdads—and several different plastic worm rigs.

Even though we kept and cleaned more fish than we usually do, there is little doubt that we released twice as many—and most of those were not small.

Our rancher host—a dead ringer for the Marlboro cowboy—politely dismissed all offers to share in our catch. So our family will just have to schedule a big Memorial Day fish fry.

Any words I string together simply fail to convey how special such a day can become in the memory of even the most jaded angler. Nevertheless, be assured of two things. First, any time brother-in-law Steve tells us he has a neat new place to take us fishing, we'll listen carefully.

And second, any time of the day or night that brother-in-law Steve invites* us to return to the water on which we spent the afternoon of Wednesday, May 25, 1988, he won't have to ask twice.

Thanks, brother-in-law. We owe you one—a very big one.

*

*A highly prized ethical tradition among honorable outdoor people throughout the Kansas Flint Hills and indeed much of the Great Plains is this: When you are an invited guest of another sportsman and you have been extended the privilege of hunting or fishing some prime new honey hole on privately owned property, the only respectable way for you to return to that place is by a future invitation or by permission from the same host.

By harsh contrast, the quickest way to get on any sportsman and/or landowner's "never again!" list is to go sneaking back with a carload of buddies for a little sleazy poaching. Among most rural Midwesterners, a reputation for honorable, respectful outdoor sporting behavior is earned with the passage of time and consistent mutual respect and decency. Sadly, a nagging percentage of unsporting blokes seem to find ways to lose access privileges and others' respect in the short span of one or two stupid, unlawful and/or unsafe decisions.

Chapter 15

In Remembrance of Christopher

Memorial Day 1989

Several days had passed with little more than an occasional thought about my oldest son, Chris. Then I stepped up and over the crest of a pond dam and scanned this cool, clear jewel glistening in the almost hushed twilight of a golden evening in mid-May, just the way he and I had shared it during dozens of spring escapes through much of his 21 years.

My gut wrenched from the twisting knife that wasn't there. I dropped to a knee and felt the hot tears come.

It has been seven months now and the tears don't come as often. But I still don't know how anyone copes with the death of a child. How does a man deal with the death of a son with whom he has shared the challenges of helping each other grow up—and the joys, so many joys—including lots of outdoor memories?

It seems especially tough when the memories are triggered by the most innocent of objects and events: opening a closet door and catching a greasy old baseball cap as it slips off a top shelf, a hat that he wore to a part-time Goodyear tire shop job before starting college; walking up behind a student crossing the university campus—a kid with the exact same complexion, same build, same color and texture of hair, same smiling blue eyes—fighting to keep from embarrassing him and myself by staring and then, giving in, introducing myself, fumbling to explain and to apologize for staring; and, of course, stepping over that pond dam where Chris caught his first keepin'-size bass at the ripe old age of 5 years.

I find it hard to believe well-meaning friends who say the pain will subside. Nevertheless, I can share a few things that seem to ease the anguish a bit, just in case it might help some fellow struggler endure a similar loss.

First, I acknowledge the tragedy.

Sometimes when I least expect it, something sparks grief as intense as if I'd just received the phone call from a Washington state trooper telling about the fog-shrouded car wreck. The pond dam incident is an example. A week before, it was the sun setting just beyond a Flint Hills horizon.

These little moments tend to run their course. I snap back to today's world and come to grips with the cold fact that Chris is dead. He is gone. Fellow travelers through this life—from family, our church, the university and the extended community—helped us bury the ashes of Bryan Christopher Irwin on a cold, gray Saturday last October.

At least I can write the words now.

Second, I marvel at the number of memories of our son that remain— many through the lives and laughter of his family and friends. Others are tied to things we shared including outdoor things. There are images that will remain forever in my memory: his small hand reaching up for support from his "Grampy" Irwin as they pawed and probed a lush green Coffey County hillside for wild strawberries in June—and a pair of wide, juicy grins that confirmed the search was successful; the expression on his face that seemed to last through a long-ago evening in April after family friend Dale Hogan helped him pull in his first squirming, wiggling crappie from one of Levern Love's hillside farm ponds; the sound of an unusually quiet Chris as we rode the 20 miles home from a vast West Texas ranch where he had harvested a half-dozen doves from a windmill watering hole with a new Remington 870 pump shotgun he'd bought with savings from a summer of lawn mowing; the look of pride mixed with disbelief when his younger brother Matt outscored him on the written test for their Kansas hunter safety course the year we moved back to Emporia; the look of bewildered amazement, then pride, when his kid sister Amy shattered the first clay target ever thrown for her (and three out of the next five!); and, in more recent years as a premed student, the look of one at peace with himself and the world whenever he returned from fishing the crystal-clear water in a favorite old stone quarry in Osage County.

Finally, what seems to provide the most healing effect after the loss of this son is a renewed investment in the lives of his survivors. Without wallowing in an unhealthy, melancholy distortion of his image, the best of Chris seems to be reflected in the time we spend with his brothers and his sister—Matt, Eric and Amy—his extended family, and scattered visits with his friends.

You see, the grin on the face of our youngest, 8-year-old Eric, two summers back when he caught his first bass was remarkably similar to the recent grin on 20-year-old Matt's face when he hefted a whopping 8-inch bass from that same old stone quarry—and both are flashbacks to that crappie-catching grin Dale Hogan and I remember from so long ago.

Or there's the simple, uncluttered satisfaction that comes with spending a cool summer evening teaching Amy to service the reliable little VW Bug she'll drive back to college in the fall. And there's the Amy who is a stronger, classier, more mature young lady than she was that cold, gray Saturday last October.

We'll never recover completely from our loss of Chris, but we'll be eternally grateful to have shared in his life and, paraphrasing the poet James Kavanaugh, "grateful above all … that he walked easy on the earth."

Part Three: Summer Overview

Ah, June: the month of great fly-rod and top-water fishing in our farm ponds, creek pools and small watershed lakes for pan fish and heart-stopping bass strikes!

Summer is a time for back-to-basics fishing with kids—yours or your neighbor's—and in chapter 18 you'll get a glance at how you can do it through agencies like Big Brothers Big Sisters. Summer's a great time to touch base with (and learn something of value from) the veteran anglers in our lives—treasures like Emporia's Noel Lyons.

By late July and August we're float-tube fishing early and late to beat the heat or staying home to get caught up on house, lawn and garden chores before late-August scouting for mourning doves.

Veteran angler Noel Lyons guides a tour through his vast tackle collection. (See chapter 19.)

Chapter 16

Bait Shop Enriches Treasure Hunt

June 1990

During a recent spring fever–laced lunch break, Kirk Dabbs was standing in the Tackle Box, a cozy little bait-and-tackle shop on south Commercial Street in Emporia, Kansas. He was waiting in line while owner George Stuck was selling live minnows and other baits to three or four of his regulars.

Idly passing the time, Kirk surveyed the place, scanning a wall covered with faded photos: here, local concrete finisher Frank Lehnherr muscling a double-arm span stringer with a half-dozen gorgeous channel catfish; there, a silver-haired grandma with what might be a grandson, hoisting a memorable string of crappie; a more recent picture of a trophy bass with a mouth exceeded in width only by the grin on a wholesome-pretty, freckle-faced teen straining to hold up her lunker bass for the camera … and so on.

On the yellowed wall just right of the cash register, among the sales display cards for Shyster, Mepps, and Bass Buster spinning lures, was a lone transparent plastic box, Scotch-taped to the cracking paint, with one of those old minnow-shaped plugs in it. Kirk reached up, took the box down, blew off a layer of dust and peeled away the brittle tape. The illustrations and the writing on the outside of the box were a little faded, but the contents were unmistakable.

Sure enough, a small green slip of paper inside, under the lure, confirmed his suspicions: this was a genuine Swimmin' Minnow. The slip of paper said, "Wt. ½ oz; Large Size; Deep Runner—Same fast action on slow retrieve as our popular ¼-oz size; Runs deeper where the big ones stay; Trolls to a depth of 10 ft. or more; Won't twist line; Needle-point hooks; Attractive fish-getting patterns. Designed and manufactured exclusively by Tackle Industries, Shreveport, Louisiana."

As Kirk held it in his hand, the plug triggered instant memories of one he'd had before snagging it on submerged tree roots and losing it years before. This one had a dull-green top, silver sides, and red in the front "mouth" area, with two treble hooks attached to the lure's belly. In other words, it looked like a 2-inch green sunfish—favorite food of the largemouth bass.

And Kirk had to have it!

If there ever was a price marked on the box, it had long since peeled off or faded. As the last of the minnow buyers left through the squeaky screen door, Kirk held up the small box and asked, "Got any more dusty old lures like this one?"

"Nope," George replied. "That old crankbait is probably the only thing of any value from a whole box of junk tackle left behind by the previous owner." Kirk's shoulders slumped in mild disappointment.

The two men agreed on a price for the old plug. Kirk paid for it, as well as a rod tip replacement he'd scheduled with George the week before, and left the shop a happy man-boy.

In the days that have followed, Kirk's quiet joy over finding the vintage lure has been justified—several times over. And, "Oh yeah! It catches bass," he reported.

"Remember that big watershed pond up toward Burdick that we used to fish? Couple days ago, I phoned Ol' Mac. Danged if he ain't still alive and well, crusty as ever, but he says we still got clearance to fish the place.

"I was on that water at sunrise the next day," he continued. "I tied on that Swimmin' Minnow, cast it out and counted it down for about six seconds—nothin'. The second cast I counted down, raised, then lowered my rod tip; the line jerked sideways, and I set the hook on the biggest bass of my life! I know 'cause she broke the surface, did a badass tail dance, shakin' her head like crazy, and flipped that plug loose—more my bad landing technique than bad tackle. For a minute or two I thought I was gonna puke.

"But you know what? Before the sun climbed above those old oak trees along the east shoreline, that Swimmin' Minnow nailed four more bass that my spring scale pegged between 4 and 6 pounds." With a muffled chuckle, Kirk added, "There I was, sittin' in my float-tube rig, catchin' beautiful bass, and the biggest rascal was towin' me around in a circle before I finally got it landed, unhooked and weighed!

"You shoulda been there. That bass plug has earned itself a whole new meaning for the name 'classic.'"

Just as he started to walk away with the hint of a shy-but-silly grin pasted on his face, Kirk looked back over his shoulder and said, "Oh yeah … Mac asked if you'd be comin' back with me."

✳

Postscript: We're convinced Kirk's prized lure was pretty old, because there was no zip code included in the box with the Shreveport address for Tackle Industries. And a quick check with telephone directory assistance in Shreveport revealed no listing for a Tackle Industries.

Be assured I'll keep you posted as we continue this adventure. If lures like Kirk's are still available—even if patent and production rights have been purchased by another company and the lures are being sold under another brand name—I'll let you know, because dedicated anglers deserve at least one Swimmin' Minnow in their tackle box.

Post-Postscript (2014): Current marketing technology has revolutionized the collecting of vintage everything (you fill in the blank), including old fishing tackle. For example, after I logged on to eBay.com this morning and typed "Swimmin' Minnow fishing lures" into the search space, dozens of these old lures and at least as many of a vintage competitor,

Pico Perch, flashed up and down the screen. Talk about happy scrolling! More good news: Except for truly rare collector grades, most of these vintage lures are so reasonably priced (a few bucks) that the shipping charges commonly exceed the asking price. And the supply seems plentiful enough to encourage us old plug flingers to keep right on fishing with them so we can rediscover how potent they can be.

Kirk's last word of encouragement might be "Whatever vintage fishing gear catches your fancy, keep checkin' those local mom-and-pop bait-and-tackle shops."

Happy collecting—for enriched fishing.

Chapter 17

For Kansas Fishing, Small Is Good

June 1991 and 2015

Many of us have enjoyed a lifelong love affair with farm ponds and small creeks. Given the choice of fishing a federal reservoir, a state fishing lake, a river, a creek or a farm pond, we'll pick the pond or the creek nine of 10 times. We like working and playing around small waters—for several reasons.

First, fishing a series of quiet pools along nearby creeks, as well as a surprising number of native tallgrass-filtered farm ponds, doesn't require a $29,000 bass boat equipped with enough electronics to embarrass the top brass at NASA's space flight control center. Let's face it, for those who've never developed (and therefore have no interest in) sharpening intuitive fish-stalking skills, there are boats nowadays with hardware (and software) that will sample the oxygen content, temperature and pH of surrounding water, take a computer-enhanced, sonar-generated picture of the contours of the bottom and the adjacent shoreline, and provide a hard-copy printout, complete with little fish-shaped blips showing where the big ones are suspended: 1.87 meters below the surface, 23 meters east-northeast of the overpadded, orthopedically correct swivel chair in which you're ~~napping~~ sitting.

If your craft (or cell phone) also happens to be equipped with one of those angler's color-selector apps, all you have left to decide is which lure from your three suitcase-size tackle boxes you'd like to throw toward the east-northeast. On a large, unfamiliar lake, you may even be able to convince your fishing guide to do the casting, the catching, the cleaning, and the stuffing of your trophy. You won't have to lift a finger.

There's a downside to this, of course. If you don't buy the big boat, you may not need the $3,000 trailer or the $45,000 GMC Suburban, Ford Explorer or double-cab Dodge Ram pickup equipped with towing package and four-wheel drive to tow it from lake to lake.

I know. It gets pretty depressing after a while, huh?

The second reason we love ponds and creeks has to do with why we fish them: to catch fish. And it gets better, especially for those with busy lives. If the fish are there and are biting, you'll most likely confirm that on small water within the first 10 minutes. Furthermore, if it's a bad day and they're not biting, you can close up your shirt-pocket tackle pack and go to another creek or pond—and keep doing this till you find where they are biting—or you quit, go home and mow the lawn or help your kids finish building that tree house.

Some of your most memorable fishing trips can consume less than an hour's time from start to finish, commute and all. Yet, if you can stay longer, it really is a win-win!

A third attribute of small waters is that they are great places to introduce (or to reintroduce) youngsters of all ages to the simple joys of fishing and being outdoors. Two weekends back, three families of us watched five kids under the age of 10 go nuts with the excitement generated by catching a few hand-size bluegill and green sunfish. Their tackle consisted of cane poles, lines, bobbers, a hook, and worms they helped Grandpa dig up behind the barn.

We packed a picnic supper. We flipped ants off of our sandwiches and chips, spilled pop on the tailgate of Grandpa's pickup, and watched another picture-postcard sun settle low over a beautiful Flint Hills farm pond.

There were no tidal waves from powerboats blasting us off of our limestone shoreline. There were no boom boxes throbbing hard rock across the water. There were no frantic races to the nearest hospital emergency room to sew up a shoreline-wading child's foot—sliced by a discarded broken bottle. There wasn't another human being within a mile.

When those five children become grandparents, that trip to the pond will be part of their personal bank of treasured memories. Believe it.

Closing thoughts: We acknowledge those who will continue to love big boats and big-water sports—from former presidents to tournament Bassmasters to the casual weekend angler. Any healthy outdoor recreation that helps us relieve the pressures and stress of life and maybe even elevate our awareness and appreciation for the wealth of natural resources around us is worth the effort.

But the mathematics of fishing across much of the Midwest is pretty compelling. In Kansas alone, we have 26 major reservoirs. We have 40-some state fishing lakes. Meanwhile, we have more than 100,000 farm ponds and no idea how many small creeks.

So when you consider the convenience, the cost, and the benefits enjoyed by young and old, small waters are a big resource.

Float-tubing small water at dusk with fly rod and
popping bugs can spike anglers' heart rate.

Chapter 18

Kids and Fish Steal Big
Brothers Big Sisters Show

June 2013

On the evening of Tuesday, June 18, the lives of almost two dozen Lyon County, Kansas, youngsters, 4 to 12 years old, were enriched in ways some of us might have taken for granted when we were their age. Each child was matched up in a near-one-to-one arrangement with an adult for an evening of "bobber and worm" fishing, complete with hot dogs and s'mores roasted over wood coals with all the trimmings, and still more fishing!

The event, held on the northeast shore of Lyon County State Fishing Lake near Reading, was hosted by the Flint Hills chapter of Big Brothers Big Sisters (BBBS) and by a Wichita-based national organization, Pass It On – Outdoor Mentors.

Andrea Lundgren, the local BBBS director, explained that the fishing party was primarily intended to reach BBBS children who (1) had not yet been matched up with a Big Brother or a Big Sister, and (2) were interested in going fishing (some for the first time) with an adult.

Mike Christenson, the CEO and driving force behind Pass It On – Outdoor Mentors, who coordinates and directs similar events statewide, had contacted leaders of several local wildlife conservation chapters (National Wild Turkey Federation, Pheasants Forever/Quail Forever, Quail and Upland Wildlife

Federation), asking them to recruit local anglers who'd like to take a kid fishing. (See appendix.)

The fun began just minutes after one of those "here one minute, gone the next" late-afternoon thunder showers blew through. From the lakeside WPA-vintage limestone shelter house, Christenson and Lundgren matched each of the 20 or so children with a snazzy fishing rod and a push-button reel already rigged with hook, line, split-shot sinker and colorful bobber, an individual Styro-cube of fat, wiggly earthworms, and an adult volunteer fishing coach.

Anything else we might write or say about the evening pales in comparison with the patience, focused attention, excitement and joy expressed by two dozen kids throughout the next couple of hours. We can only offer a few photos as supporting evidence.

This is Peyton, one of the first to catch a fish; she may have caught the most, and by evening's end she had baited her own hook, cast, caught, unhooked and strung enough pan fish to be willing to coach the next group of kids!

It's tough to tell who's best at striking a pose—Mason or his first catch!

Talk about patience! Robert was perhaps the last to hook one. No matter, because he got a chuckle out of catching a fish that was almost shorter than the worm on his hook.

*Every fishing party, Scout troop and primary school classroom
needs an Eli. Who knew one of the youngest and most patient
members of the Big Brothers Big Sisters fishing class would
take seriously our co-host Mike Christenson's comical tip for
how to keep your earthworm bait extra moist (and tasty!)?*

Chapter 19

Local Bass Angler Exhibits Vintage Tackle Treasures

June 2011

Noel Lyons knows fishing tackle. A lifelong small-water angler, he collects, displays, and still enjoys catching bass with vintage fishing rods, reels and all manner of related fishing gear.

Using every available square foot of the floor, walls and ceiling of a spacious second-floor mega loft above a detached double garage and a workshop next to his shady, well-tended home on East Logan Avenue in south Emporia, Lyons has created his own fishing tackle museum: an open-space loft filled to overflowing with the largest private assemblage of artificial lures, rods, reels and accessories this wide-eyed writer has ever seen in one location.

Following his retirement in 1993 after 31 years as a lineman and cable repairman with Bell Telephone, Lyons became a regular at area yard sales and auctions, always with a keen eye for modern and vintage fishing tackle used for spinning, spin casting, bait casting and fly fishing. In the ensuing years, he has accumulated, puttered with, lovingly repaired/restored, and cleverly and attractively displayed hundreds of lures, rods, reels and an equally amazing variety of related accessories spanning more than two centuries of angling.

Noel Lyons relaxes near the west wall, ceiling and floor displays of his vintage fishing tackle collection. And he has a colorful story to tell about each acquisition.

While Lyons is the first to admit his displays are not professionally cataloged and labeled, veteran anglers will note some rare, limited-production—even one-of-a-kind and/or homemade—lures and gadgets in exhibit cases, framed wall and ceiling displays, and free-standing floor display racks. But it is the variety and sheer number of items that impress visitors as they step through the loft door at the top of an outdoor wooden staircase.

And if you have the time and the good judgment to listen, Lyons will treat you to the stories and history of many of his holdings.

Speaking with quiet modesty and a twinkle in his eye, Lyons says, "I call the place my junkyard, but if a person likes to fish—or maybe even for some who don't—there's probably something here they'd enjoy seeing."

Up to now, most visitors to Lyons' amazing collection have been family, friends and fishin' buddies. But he says, "I'd enjoy showing my junkyard to anyone who'll check with me in advance." (Translation: Catch him between trips to area yard sales, auctions and bass ponds?) And if you're really lucky, the welcoming committee might include Lyons' wife, Vickie; granddaughters Melanie and Courtney; and, for sure, Lyons' joined-at-the-hip shadow, the lovable old Lab Obedye.

Another hidden Flint Hills treasure ...

*

Postscript: As of this 2015 writing, Noel Lyons' beloved Labrador retriever, Obedye, has died. Lyons reluctantly acknowledges he's "not getting any younger" and is considering selling the entire tackle collection—preferably as one complete package rather than piecing it out a few items at a time. (See the appendix for contact information.)

Lyons answers endless questions while sharing a treasure of stories about his tackle collection.

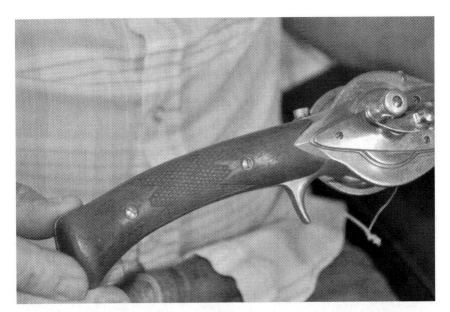

Note the hand-checkered walnut on this rare Hurd Bait Caster rig, circa late 1940s. Lyons recently learned from another collector that the steel casting rods in these rigs were skillfully crafted from military surplus salvage of the radio antennae from Sherman battle tanks used in World War II.

Chapter 20

Fish the Cool and Beat the Heat

July 2011

Though we'd both logged float-tube fishing into our cell phone calendars, neither of us could get away in the optimum cool of early morning a week or two back. Bill Hartman is only semiretired from heating, cooling and caring for buildings on the Emporia State University campus. Workplace obligations still trump outdoor fun and frolic.

So, using Hartman's unwillingness to get himself fired prematurely, I filled the morning with puttering chores and yard work before the midday solar cooker that is our backyard drove me inside to air-conditioning and a late lunch.

At 3:30, a phone call from Bill shattered a short, sweet nap and propelled me to the garage. And there was my friend, standing in front of my open garage door, having already loaded most of my float-tube gear and patiently glancing at his wristwatch. With fly rods and gear, snacks and water bottles in tow, we rattled our way over 35 miles of alternating hot asphalt and dusty gravel deep into the patchwork landscape of native Kansas pasture, fresh-cut wheat stubble, and the rolling woodland bowels of eastern Greenwood County.

It was still on the lingering edge of hot in the open sun as we drove through and then closed the last of three pasture gates. As we followed the two-track across the top of a high, narrow dam that spans the deep cut between two wooded slopes, the lengthening afternoon shadows on the west shoreline of a half mile-long, blue-green watershed lake were beckoning.

Bill said, "You'll recognize this as a place we fished on an Indian summer afternoon last October." As we both remembered it, we'd earned every strike we got that day—a dozen or so fat, palm-size bluegills. And then, in that optimistic tone host anglers love to take when they start the casting, he added, "The bluegills are still here, some even bigger and fatter, but we've also taken some nice bass and crappie from this water."

After getting all our gear and ourselves afloat in our tube rigs, we split up—Bill casting and paddling his way up the east shore to the north end and then slowly drifting in the slightest of breezes down the shady west side. Meanwhile, I flippered my way toward the southwest corner and floated into the shadows of cottonwood, elm, ash and willow.

After using a variety of weighted flies and catching a few nice bluegill and bright-orange-bellied pumpkinseeds during the first hour or so, both of us independently settled on tiny, brightly colored popping bugs to try for some late-afternoon surface action.

Few outdoor experiences can spike your pulse the way a 1-pound black bass can as it erupts from a shaded shoreline pool, inhales that teeny popper and goes airborne in a 2-foot arc only to hit the water swimming at top speed to left, right and then straight down—bending your fly rod in a wavering arc of its own. For each of us to have that thrill within 50 yards and two or three casts of each other and land bass in the 2-pound range was, uh, "worth the price of the ticket," as they say in slick-paper outdoor magazines.

Was this the heart-stopping feeding frenzy on a sunbathed farm pond in late March or early April? No.

We were patiently doing what small-water anglers in the Flint Hills have to do to catch fish in the heat of midsummer. If you can be on the water between dawn and 9 a.m. and/or between 6 p.m. and "dark-thirty," you can catch fish from clear, clean, tallgrass-filtered waters—even in midsummer.

If your worldly responsibilities or sleeping preferences keep you grounded during the early morning hours, slip out after work and dinner with the family. There's still enough twilight to tie a popping bug to 6-pound test leader at 9 p.m. in July.

And those Flint Hills sunsets might even prompt you to invite a significant other. But don't come to us for help if the pungency of your bug repellent squelches the charm of your picnic blanket and chilled wine.

Fly fishing guide and the author's occasional partner in outdoor frolic, this is Bill Hartman at his best.

Chapter 21

Managing Wheat Stubble for More Doves

July 2012

Like the sleek, silent aerial ghosts they are, three doves slipped through a gap in the tree line bordering the far side of our field and curved their flight in a right-to-left arc 30 yards in front of the shaded stool where professor friend and veteran bird hunter Dale Hogan was perched and waiting. In one continuous motion, he rose from his inverted five-gallon bucket, shouldered his over/under 12 gauge, swung through the birds' flight path and, with the sound-over-distance delay from our vantage point across the field, we watched two birds fall at the same time we heard the muffled *"pop, pop!"*

Ten minutes later, Dale met his son Allan and me back at his old station wagon. A stashing of gear, a brief exchange of cheers and jeers for shots well made plus a rehash of our usual spectacular misses, and a quick count of our collective birds revealed another memorable opening day for mourning doves taken over disked Lyon County wheat stubble.

That memory is 50 years old. Yet it is no less clear than the decades of similar memories from intervening years and season-opening weekends—stretching from cut-over grain fields in the Rio Grande valley of deep South Texas to the

Pecos River basin of West Texas to the stubble fields across creek and river basins throughout the Flint Hills of Kansas.

Fast-forward to today. Recent drives along local country roads and highways have been encouraging. We've seen more post-harvest wheat stubble fields than in recent summers. This bodes well for the September mourning dove season. Doves have always been drawn to freshly harvested grain fields, and wheat stubble is near the top of their list.

To increase the probability that area wheat farmers can host as many doves as possible for the family and friends they invite for those traditional Labor Day weekend shoots of early fall, we pass along some wheat-field management tips from wildlife and agricultural agencies near and far.

"To ensure that wheat in your stubble field or food plot is available for doves, it should be disturbed in some way. You can mow, hay, burn or disk, or any combination of the four," suggests an unnamed habitat specialist on a website at the Iowa Department of Natural Resources. (See appendix.)

Other state agencies and wildlife conservation groups agree. A recent rainy-day search through my bookshelves led me to scan the Wildlife Management Institute book "Ecology and Management of the Mourning Dove" (Baskett, 1993). Chapter 28, headed "Shooting Field Management," explains, "Managers of public land and private hunt clubs, farmers and dove hunters have developed methods and techniques to manipulate [grain] crop residues and specific plantings to provide the important combination of bare ground and abundant small seeds. Any field that is somehow managed to enhance its attractiveness to doves (other than illegal baiting) must possess at least one of the essential ingredients of dove habitat (food, water, shelter and some open ground) and be in proximity to the others."

Most agricultural agencies and wildlife conservation organizations with online or printed publications on managing land for doves suggest mowing strips through wheat stubble or food plots as a proven dove attractor. If you mow, make sure not too much wheat straw is on the ground so doves can get to the grain.

In some years, if there is too much straw, burning patches, strips or irregular parts of the cut/dried straw about two weeks before the season opens is recommended. However, burning requires the usual serious precautions (alerting neighboring farmers, rural and volunteer fire departments). If you do burn, you'll want to do it on a day when wind is slight and there is enough humidity so the straw doesn't burn too hot and completely consume the wheat seeds.

If you choose not to burn strips or patches, another alternative is to windrow mowed wheat stubble to open up more ground. And baling some of the windrows and leaving the bales spaced around the field is a good way to provide cover for hunters.

*

As in that long-ago hunt with the Hogans, some of my most memorable dove shoots have been over freshly disked wheat (and other grain crop) stubble. Disking strips within a field of grain stubble is a great way to provide food across the surface of bare soil and is very attractive to doves.

I'm hoping that area farmers who still have some undisturbed wheat stubble from summer's harvest will find one or more of the above dove-management tools compatible with their crop rotation plans.

Chapter 22

Why Bird Hunters' Health
Improves in Late August

August 2011

The dawn sky was overcast. No greeting-card sunrise this day. Yet there they were, the very critters we hoped to find when we took to this country road. At ground level in front of us, along the top wires of fences, and on overhead power lines, we spotted mourning doves—scads of 'em!

Dozens of doves perched along one quarter-mile stretch of power lines bordering a cornfield that had been cut and shredded for silage just the afternoon before. They'd flush from the lines and fences only briefly as our German shorthair Shani and I cruised slowly by on a scouting mission. Some doves settled right back on their perches, while others winged their way into the adjacent fields in search of waste grain and weed seeds scattered by the previous day's crop chopping.

All this occurred along the same road where a drive-by two days before had revealed little bird traffic, only the occasional flight of three or four doves (most probably summer-resident mating pairs and their one or two latest hatchlings) sharing a morning commuter flight from roost to feed fields and water holes.

"Why all the excitement?" you ask.

Perhaps it's because, having endured the dog days of August, we're on the cusp of a series of annual seasons for hunting harvestable surpluses of Kansas game birds—which traditionally begins on September 1 with mourning doves.

Maybe some of our preseason excitement comes from having missed out on competitive trap shooting or any other form of busting clay targets this summer, and like many Great Plains bird hunters, we cleaned and stored our bird guns after last January's wrap-up hunts for quail and pheasant. So, seeing all those doves a few days ago, staging and gorging on weed and seed grains as they prepared to embark on their annual migration through Oklahoma, Texas, and points south, has helped us forget all those recent days of scorching heat indexes and heightened our anticipation for the wings of autumn.

Our enthusiasm also gets support from decades of field studies, call counts and nesting success surveys that show mourning doves are nearly unique among all the birds of North, Central and South America in that their geographic distribution and population numbers have grown substantially in response to the advances of the human species and the ever-expanding food grains we plant and harvest each year.

U.S. Fish and Wildlife estimates of the number of mourning doves in the lower 48 states over the last decade have ranged between 250 million and 400 million. Nesting pairs of Kansas doves—year-round residents and the majority that migrate each spring—lay and hatch just one or two eggs in a 23- to 25-day nesting/brooding cycle, but may complete two or even three cycles between March and the end of July. The longer breeding seasons in Oklahoma and Texas may support up to five successful nesting cycles for doves.

So cruise a few country roads in search of concentrations of these abundant sporting game birds, check with nearby farmhouses for the appropriate person to contact for legal access, limber up your shooting eye with a friend or two and a carton of hand-thrown or gun-club clay targets, update any license needed, and don't forget the Harvest Inventory Program stamp required of hunters of all migratory game birds.

Worst-case scenario: Your scouting is a bust or you find concentrations of birds but can't locate the landowner or lessee to secure the necessary legal permission. Okay, back to the website for the fish and game department in the state where you'll be hunting. (See appendix.) Search for details on areas specially managed for doves. In Kansas, get on the website kdwpt.state.ks.us/ and click Hunting/Migratory Birds/Doves/ Managed Hunting Areas for details on the nearest managed dove area.

An August news release from the Kansas Department of Wildlife, Parks and Tourism says, "While a blistering summer may have punished crops and people, mourning doves seem to thrive in hot, dry weather. Reports from many parts of the state suggest ample numbers of this elusive, fast-flying quarry." You can watch a two-minute dove-scouting video and check on the dates, details and bag limits in the fall and winter hunting regulations, available on the department's website.

My 50-plus dove seasons have included taking lots of youngsters of all ages on their first dove hunt (or the first one in a long time), and at some point during the drive home almost all of them have asked some variation on the question, "When can we do this again?"

May it be ever thus for you and yours.

Late-August gravel-road and grain-field scouting can increase September success with your annual dove harvest.

Chapter 23

Confessions of a Terminally Addicted Dove Hunter

August 1997

Several of us charter members of the local chapter of the Society for Tragically Underachieving Dove Shooters (STUDS) have been so disillusioned by the last few dove seasons that we weren't all that excited as this year's opening day approached. What we've experienced the first week of the last three seasons is a single weekend, maybe two, of encouraging numbers of birds. Then we brag a little too much or go on about how many birds were strafing our field and about how great the shooting was. We talk one or two carloads of relatives and friends into returning to the same field for a second or third sampling of this early-autumn sporting tradition, and *poof!* The doves have all gone south—literally.

So our son Eric—high school senior and weekend chef's apprentice at the beautifully restored Grande Hotel and Grill in Cottonwood Falls—caught us off guard this past week. From his sprawled-the-full-length-of-the-couch position in our family room, he raised himself on one elbow and asked, "Hey Dad! If I invite Chad and Jarrod and a couple more friends out for a dove hunt this week or next, can you take us?"

"Well, er … uh … uh … duh," I responded in my less-than-convincing hunting-guide fashion. Then I recovered and offered, "Gosh, Eric, except for driving different country roads to and from the university each morning and evening for the past few days, I haven't done my usual, irrepressibly optimistic, five-county preseason scouting, but I'll do a little checking around, and you can talk to your grandpa and Uncle Steve. We should be able to come up with something."

Two evenings later, Eric and I drove down a gravel road within a few miles of our home in the Flint Hills, checking crop rotations on each side of the road and scanning power lines and fences for gatherings of doves. Ed Aeschliman, a neighbor we've done some bird-dog business with, was just pulling out of an 80-acre field after disking bare strips in the wheat stubble on his old red International Harvester tractor.

Doves were scattered along the power lines and the top strand of wire fence around his field and in shady spots along the road. Ed shut off his tractor and wandered over to our pickup with a big, dusty grin. "I just barely got this patch ready in time for tomorrow's opener," he said. "I'm guessin' you've already noted that I left the terraces standing in tall grass and sunflowers—at least 'til we git done usin' 'em for shady cover. Can you two make it out at sun-up tomorrow?"

I assured Ed I could hunt for an hour or so before teaching my first morning class and added that Eric and a few friends would like to come out later in the week. He leaned into the pickup cab, looked straight at Eric and said, "You're welcome to hunt here, son. Bring as many safety-conscious bird hunters as you can—the more the better to spread yourselves out around one or two of the terraced strips and that'll help keep the birds stirred up and shuffling among you." Then, on his walk back to the old tractor, he pivoted around to add, "And remind your buddies that they need to buy their annual HIP migratory bird hunters' stamp and carry it with their license."

That evening there was renewed excitement around our house. The family room was filled with the classic fragrance of Hoppe's No. 9 gun-cleaning solvent as I stroked the receiver of a vintage 16-gauge Remington Model 31 pump. I stayed awake through all of the 10 o'clock news and weather report just to make sure there would be no slip-ups on the official time for the opener's sunrise. Then I drifted off to sleep reading a Charley Waterman dove-hunting article in a decade-old issue of Wing and Shot.

At dawn's muted light, I was seated on a camo folding stool in some shoulder-high sunflowers along the wheat stubble's west border. Ordinarily that position would have me squinting into the sunrise, but there was a cloud bank in the east. So I kept glancing at my watch to determine when it was legal to shoot at the gray-feathered speedsters that had been silently settling into the field since I eased out of the old green pickup, found my spot and sat down.

Five minutes into this brand-new season, there were two doves in my game bag as Ed parked his old Ford and shuffled along a weedy terrace 300 yards northeast of me. Neither of us had much time for the morning part of this opener as there were still more occupational responsibilities tugging at our day. But with barely an hour of alternating periods of fast shooting and a few short lulls in the action, we met at Ed's truck and took inventory.

Ed had not been sitting in the high-traffic lane that I enjoyed, but he laid out seven doves he'd dropped and softly mumbled, "Shoulda had eight; missed one—a hard-right crosser when I first sat in the weeds." For the uninitiated, that's exceptional dove shooting. The shot-shell manufacturers at Winchester, Remington and Federal estimate it takes the average dove hunter six to 10 shots for each bird bagged.

One bird short of the daily limit myself (don't ask how many spectacular misses were interspersed among those birds brought to hand), I thanked our neighbor/host for the privilege. I dashed home, cleaned my birds, bagged and refrigerated them, showered, shaved and drove to my nine o'clock class.

On my way to campus, I drove back past the wheat stubble and offered a simple, silent thank-you to Mother Earth and to Ed for providing 80 acres of Great Plains habitat that, for many seasons, has appealed to the brood-rearing needs and migratory behavior of so many mourning doves.

The next evening the doves were still there. Hunting solo, with no other hunters scattered around the field, I decided to walk the length of the 80 acres and to update myself on this year's rendition of the landscape. Weedy terraces cut across the property from southeast to northwest, outlining strips of stubble, a promising set-up for jump shooting. There were doves everywhere as I moved along, mostly flushing well out of shooting range, of course. At the north end of some of the strips, the birds fanned out in waves ahead of me—flocks of 20 and more.

Just often enough to keep me focused, errant doves flew within range. Some got scratched, but more flew on unscathed. It was clear that this field lends itself to scattering a group of hunters at safe intervals around its perimeter, like the legendary plantation dove shoots of the American South.

Although I hoped Eric and his friends and/or my father-in-law and other family members would get to enjoy a shoot here before one of those chilly Labor Day thunderstorms moved through and spooked most of the birds on south, I was prepared for the likelihood that all those birds would be here today, gone tomorrow.

Who knows? Maybe that's part of the sporting charm of the first week or two of mourning dove season in Kansas. Maybe it's enough just to be reassured that Mother Earth has once again produced a harvestable surplus—and that another bird season is here.

Part Four: Autumn Overview

The climate from mid-September through early November across our slice of the Great Plains typically lends itself well to another dove shoot or two, which leads into the early season for our native grouse, the greater prairie chicken, and forays into the Nebraska Sand Hills for sharp-tail grouse and more chickens. Then the harvest of pheasants in Kansas, Nebraska and the Dakotas beckons.

Some of our small- and big-water anglers insist it is this time of year when the quality of fishing is at its best. The crowds are back to work and school; the turbulence of the thunderstorm season has passed; those trolling past the docks and the lakeshore cabins find the water quiet and peaceful, with the infrequent sound of the season's last mowing of a small patch of lawn or of hammers and saws weatherproofing a family's summer nest for the coming winter.

This is prized destination habitat for hunters of the prairie grouse. And scattered windmill water tanks can provide cooling refreshment for hunters and dogs. (See chapter 26.)

Chapter 24

Tallgrass Search for an Original American Native

September 1997

The windswept grass swayed hypnotically before them as far as the eye could see. Traversing gentle rises between shallow ravines, Kirk and his two old Brittanys had eased their way into the wind in a wide, quartering pattern that would cross hundreds of acres of grass. They were in search of greater prairie chickens in the Kansas Flint Hills.

It was late September. The early season for chickens was in its second week and would continue until mid-October. This is a great time of year for hunter and dog to stretch leg muscles and lungs. Many bird stalkers in the Great Plains upland view this early chicken season as the first chance of the year to introduce a pup to scenting live native birds or to reacquaint a gray-muzzled veteran with the practice.

It was early afternoon, with air temperature in the 70s. Given a moderate south-southwest breeze, Kirk had elected to park his pickup at a cattle pen on the gravel road bordering the north edge of the property. Tossing the slender core of a tart Jonathan apple he'd snatched from a box on the back porch of his sister's farmhouse when he'd checked in with her moments before, Kirk wiped the sticky juice off of his chin and fingers with a couple of swipes on the front of his weathered hunting shirt. He buckled the old waxed canvas strap vest, slipped a pair of No. 6 shot shells into his 16-gauge double, and watched the dogs work the grass back and forth, first east, then west, at right angles to the wind.

Twelve-year-old Pete, the liver-and-white Brittany, settled into his trademark close-working pattern. Weaving back and forth as he vacuumed the bluestem and switchgrass, he gave little hint of the advancing cataracts and near total deafness that Kirk first noticed during spring and summer outings to farm ponds. Meanwhile, Lady McBess (just Bess to family, friends and seasonal hunting partners), the only pup Kirk didn't sell out of a 1992 litter of orange-on-white Brittanys, was pushing the grassy envelope but still within view—most of the time.

Kirk's strategy worked, but not until he and the dogs were within sight of the most distant corner of the pasture. A massive hedge corner post, with brace posts and cross members on either side, came into view as he and Pete crested a rolling swell in the landscape. The stout vertical lines of the weathered wooden monuments and the five horizontal strands of barbed wire that connected them were the only traces of humanity they had seen in 40 minutes of continuous walking across this tallgrass floor of just one of thousands of square miles of "big sky" Flint Hills.

At about this point Kirk realized he hadn't seen Bess in a while. Scanning 360 degrees of grass with no sight of her, he and Pete backtracked their last hundred yards and found her on solid point. She was just downwind from a scrubby little patch of the noxious, invasive woody forb *Sericea lespedeza*. Pete slithered in behind her in a half-crouched point of honor.

Kirk took two more steps at right angles to the dogs, and three prairie chickens were airborne. His 16-gauge swung through the flight path of the bird on the left, the improved cylinder barrel barked into the wind, the bird crumpled and Bess was on it. Though clearly a young bird of the current year's hatch, this critter was a lot larger than the resident quail Bess was used to retrieving. So after fussing with it for a few seconds and with some patient encouragement from Kirk, she managed to get it about halfway to her master, dropped it in the grass and looked up at him as if to say, "Hey! I've done my part. If you want this bird, come and get it."

Less than a minute later, Pete showed some "birdy" posturing. Then Bess moved in shoulder to shoulder with him, and both dogs froze like a Frederic Remington sculpture. A single bird flushed at Kirk's advance, quartering away in the direction of a small pond they had skirted earlier. The 1-ounce charge of No. 6 shot served its intended purpose, and the bird fell to the grass.

Greater prairie chicken populations in the Kansas Flint Hills region and in the Sand Hills of Nebraska have stabilized to produce a modest harvestable surplus that both states' fish and game agencies consider sufficient to allow a moderate season and bag limit. Kirk elected to make this pair his limit for the year.

Close examination revealed this, too, was a young chicken. Its tail feathers were short, without the more conspicuous barred pattern of adult females or the dark russet tail feathers of adult males. And both birds looked and felt noticeably shy of the 2-plus pounds mature birds amass.

During the long but more direct route back to the pickup, a modest flock of eight chickens flushed well ahead of man and dogs, and with their characteristic flap-flap-flap-flap-glide pattern, these true natives were quickly distant specks against the southwest skyline. Kirk was filled with a keen sense of what he and the dogs were so fortunate to have spent the last hour doing.

The ethics and wisdom of words attributed to the eloquent Native American Indian chief Seattle echoed in his ears: "Man did not weave the web of life; he is merely a strand in it."

How privileged we are to live and to hunt in one of planet Earth's ecosystems whose strands include harvestable numbers of upland game birds such as the greater prairie chicken. It is a privilege we must always respect, and we should make ethical choices to ensure coming generations can do the same.

Chapter 25

A Model 12 Reborn: The Joy of Dealing with People Who Love What They Do and Are Very Good at Doing It

September 2010

If the average hunter/angler were to look you in the eye and provide a true accounting of waking hours spent in anticipation of his or her next outing compared with the number of hours actually engaging in this pursuit, the relative proportions would be startling. Some of the most gratifying aspects of this treasured anticipation involve almost continuous wishing for, acquiring and, dare I suggest, fondling the tools, instruments, tackle, and gear that we use to pursue those game birds and catch those fish.

This is a story of just such an anticipatory obsession.

*

There it was, Roger's early-a.m. greeting on a golden day last June, the freshest e-mail on his screen, congratulating him for the winning bid he'd submitted late the night before.

With a clear objective in mind, he'd been monitoring this and other online auctions for several weeks, but this one was clean. This one had potential: a Winchester Model 12 pump-action 16-gauge shotgun with 28-inch barrel choke "modified." Its serial number revealed a 1959 manufacture—a mere four years before this all-American classic's 50-year production run of 2 million had drawn to a close and with it a golden era of fine industrial design, engineering and craftsmanship.

The online photos and description of the shotgun rendered it a promising candidate for refinement as Roger's project gun of the year. Placed in the talented hands of the right gunsmiths, it just might be completed in time to open the 2010 bird seasons. And of less urgency but no less importance, it might also one day become a grandson's gun of a lifetime.

Several things would have to fall neatly into place. But Roger was up for that—and was already planning how the transformation would unfold.

First, instead of having the Winchester commercially shipped barely a hundred miles from the seller in western Missouri to a licensed dealer in Emporia, Kansas, with a few phone calls and careful guidance on the necessary exchange of federal firearms paperwork from the seller and from Chad Fechter, manager of Emporia's Gun Den, a more efficient plan unfolded. Early the next morning, Roger drove to the online seller's country residence near Jamestown, Missouri, met an experienced, competent gun collector steeped in knowledge of fine shotguns with whom he completed a relaxed and pleasant exchange of cash, necessary paperwork, and a Winchester "sweet sixteen" even more pristine than online photos revealed.

Because Roger is a long-limbed and lanky guy, the next stop in this bird gun's transformation required the purchase and installation of a replacement gunstock and fore-end of longer than the original over-the-counter dimensions. And the parts had to be custom crafted from premium-grade American black walnut.

So Roger offered his thanks and a good-bye to his new friend in rural Jamestown and drove an hour farther east into Ozark lake country to the town of Warsaw to consult with a friend and trusted professional, Donnie Gemes, owner/manager of Show-Me Gunstocks. Through the years, Gemes and staff have fitted some beautiful, custom-tailored wood to several fine guns for our bird hunter friend's rangy frame.

After showing as much surprise as Roger at the like-new condition of the online auction buy, Gemes made careful measurements and then showed him samples of highly figured American black walnut gunstock blanks. More discussion ensued, and a choice was made to finish the commissioned pieces with the stock maker's recommendation: the classic Winchester Model 12 Pigeon Grade checkering pattern. A price was agreed upon, and Gemes assured Roger that the stock and fore-end slide handle would receive multiple applications of Danish oil finish and that he would be contacted in about a month to confirm that these items had been forwarded to the gunsmith of his choice for final fitting.

A hint of a smile flickered across Gemes' face when Roger told him the next leg of this day's gun-buying-and-rebuilding relay was to take a little detour on the way home to Emporia. In fact, he'd already telephoned ahead and arranged to leave the Winchester at one of America's hallowed gun-crafting institutions, Simmons Gun Shop in Olathe, Kansas, so the team of gunsmiths there could install a solid raised rib on the shotgun's original barrel "and maybe add a couple of other small, upgrading touches consistent with the period in which the gun was originally made."

Gemes' smile broadened as he replied, "Well, I'll be darned. Guess who makes and/or refinishes the custom wood Simmons installs on a lot of their clients' shotguns and rifles. Their shop and ours have worked together for years."

Though it was only minutes before closing time when Roger arrived at the Simmons Gun Shop, sales manager and front-counter contact man Larry Griffin watched and listened with interest as Roger described what he'd like the resident gunsmiths to do to upgrade the little Winchester. Griffin presented a menu of choices and their costs, and a work order was written. Roger was told that he'd get a phone call in six to eight weeks to come pick up his "new" Pigeon Grade Winchester 16.

The Flint Hills bird hunter drove home to Emporia with great excitement, and the next several weeks were filled with eager anticipation.

The Wondrous Chemistry of a Cohesive Team

Roger got the phone call from Simmons during the middle of August. I had been along for the ride when he acquired the gun following the winning online auction bid and during most of the process that followed. We are longtime bird-hunting companions. So Roger invited me to accompany him to the Simmons shop the next day to pick up the reborn Winchester. One phone call later to shop owner Jim Wright, and we had extended that trip to include a guided tour of the Simmons plant, including interviews with Wright and as many of the gunsmithing staff as might be available if not unduly interrupted in their work.

The day included everything we could have hoped for—and more. Wright and Griffin, plus the gun shop's mascot, Bogie, a handsome black Lab, greeted us with Roger's completely transformed 52-year-old Winchester—now a true collector's bird gun with stunning wood and metalwork, easily worth three times his total investment. But what made Roger's acquisition and the gun restoration even more meaningful was the give-and-take as we got acquainted with the personable and multitalented smiths who took part in the upgrading process.

Wright, who bought the Simmons Gun Shop 16 years ago from second-generation owner Ernie Simmons Jr., guided our tour of the plant, deflecting attention from himself and introducing us to a close-knit team of gunsmiths with impressive (read: who's who among Midwestern gunsmiths) credentials. With soft-spoken confidence and enthusiasm, the Simmons team members described and demonstrated their specialties in the repair, reconstruction and refinement of sporting rifles and shotguns.

Imagine having a firearm selected from your closet, cabinet or gun safe serviced and cared for by any of the following:

- Mike Griffin, the operations manager, who has brought the Simmons team and some of its machinery into the 21st century with CNC technology upgrades that, with his razor-sharp programming, can remanufacture obsolete or inferior gun parts with more uniform quality and precision than ever available before.

- John Tippin, who has been installing and perfecting ventilated sighting ribs on shotgun barrels for 41 of the Simmons shop's 65 years. Tippin and Wright took pride in telling of a time, early in the shop's history, when major firearms manufacturers, including Winchester, contracted with (and were licensed by) Simmons to install the Simmons Ventilated Rib on the company's shotguns.

- Jim Clark. How about having this man ply his 36 years of experience in repairing or constructing from scratch a new pair of barrels for your over/under or side-by-side?

- Dean Kohler, who has spent 35 years repairing rifles, shotguns (he's a Winchester Model 12 specialist!) and handguns.

- Paul Sancho, who has 15 years of diverse and creative experience in repairing and reconstructing rifles (including black powder) and pistol, AR, shotgun and barrel sets.

- Matt Bliss and Frank Judd, relative newcomers who do a fair share of the bluing, rust bluing, wood finishing and general gunsmithing.

- Reggy Jamison, the new manager of the Simmons custom shop, who builds and finishes custom double-barrel sets and does engraving and case color finishing.

After a final, grateful handshake with Jim Wright, multiple thanks all around for a terrific day, and one last friendly hand-lick from Bogie (in that order), we drove home, the happiest of campers. And we remain absolutely convinced that the attributes shared by all the people who contributed to this acquisition and upgrade—from online seller, to world-class wood workers, to master gunsmiths—are these: They show great pride in what they do to earn their living, and they are very, very good at doing it.

*This little-used 16-gauge Winchester Model 12 was
transformed by skilled gunsmiths from standard grade
to near-mint Pigeon-Grade classic bird gun.*

*Note Pigeon-Grade wood, checkering and
finish of this Model 12's fore-end.*

Chapter 26

Sharp-Tails!

September 2012

It all begins and ends with the landscape. We were less than 50 miles from the South Dakota line, a half-hour drive southwest of Valentine, Nebraska.

Kevin Church of rural Emporia, Kansas, had lured me there with inviting and challenging accounts of his years as a wildlife biologist and as a recreational hunter of two species of prairie grouse across the vast, rolling Nebraska Sand Hills.

Picture, if you can, a timeless stretch of undulating sand dunes covered with a semi-stable, healing mixture of native grasses and forbs, yucca, fruiting prickly pear cactus, woody clumps of wild berries in the ravines, and in less stable spots, blown-out bowls of granular, chalky soil and windblown sand. Every few miles there are vivid blue lakes, with just enough scattered cedar trees and cottonwoods to break up the skyline at irregular intervals. All of this occupies 20,000 square miles spread across much of the north-central and northwest regions of Nebraska.

Still not impressed? We're referring to almost 13 million acres of real estate—more area than New Hampshire and Vermont combined. And these Sand Hills are home to the largest stable populations of America's prairie grouse—sharp-tail grouse and greater prairie chicken, which produce harvestable annual surpluses.

We left Emporia on a Saturday morning in early October and 10 hours later had Kevin's camping trailer unhooked, popped up and leveled, and were enjoying his camp-stove pizza for supper at dusk in the Valentine National Wildlife Refuge.

Thanks to Kevin's career as a wildlife biologist at state conservation agencies in Kansas, Nebraska and Idaho, plus the lifetime he has spent hunting several species of grouse throughout the U.S., my three-day introduction to the pursuit of a mixed three-bird daily bag limit of sharp-tails and chickens in the breathtaking panorama of those Sand Hills already occupies a treasured place among decades of wing-shooting memories.

Each day's hunting went something like this. After coffee and a quick-but-nourishing "light" breakfast, we'd drive a remote two-track trail into the refuge's vast landscape and park next to a windmill and a water tank in some scenic location where Kevin had enjoyed successful hunts in past years. Then we'd unload his German shorthair Greta and my smallish female shorthair Shani, stoke our vests with shot shells, water bottles, granola bars, and dog-handling gear including Kevin's all-purpose control for both dogs' electronic collars plus GPS monitoring of where the dogs were in relation to us and where we were in relation to our parked vehicle.

Then, with both of us opting to carry lighter, over/under 20-gauge shotguns with fairly open (improved cylinder and modified) chokes, we'd spread out a quarter-mile or more apart from each other and strike out on generally parallel courses, working our way up and down large and small hills and along the crests of ridges connecting major dunes, with our dogs quartering back and forth before us, vacuuming the breeze for bird scent.

Our morning hunts lasted about two hours, with a much-needed noon break to rehydrate with water or a sports drink, to drive back to camp to eat a moderate lunch, and to rest our aging lungs and legs for a few minutes with bodies horizontal and eyes in at least half-closed position.

The afternoons were a repeat of the morning pattern, but in a new location and extending for three to four hours. As a Nebraska Game and Parks brochure on grouse hunting cautions, "Hunting in the early season can be very warm and conditioning of hunter and dog is important. Condition dogs during the preseason and know how to treat heatstroke before hunting in the Sand Hills." (See appendix.) Indeed, we made sure Greta and Shani got a drink of water just about every time we did.

Our bird harvest was every bit as much as we needed: Kevin rolled one prairie chicken and one sharp-tail out of that cornflower-blue Nebraska sky on our first day, and Shani and I managed a couple of young sharp-tails too. The second day's hunt produced a limit of three sharp-tails for Kevin, and I had a long, scenic walk up, down and around those hills, never in close enough range to venture a shot at several scattered singles or pairs of birds cackling their way over the top of the next dune. But on our third and last day, Lady Luck favored us with one sharp-tail in the midmorning and a second late-afternoon bird that flushed from in front of Shani's best point of the trip and launched from the long shadows of one of those curious, bowl-shaped blow-out depressions near the top of a steep hill.

Each evening as we dressed and iced down the birds for transport home, Kevin patiently instructed (then later quizzed) me on the subtle traits that distinguish young birds from old, male from female. Using that information, we filled in the survey for Nebraska Game and Parks' population studies printed on large envelopes in which we deposited one wing from each harvested bird, placing the envelopes in boxes at the entrance/exit of key hunting areas within the refuge each day. It was a productive way to say thanks for the privilege of harvesting some of nature's bounty from one of America's few remaining expanses of beautiful, rolling prairie landscape.

The author's friend, tolerant hunting partner, and Great Plains grouse authority, retired wildlife biologist Kevin Church, who logged a career of service in Kansas, Nebraska and Idaho's state game agencies, double-checks the info he recorded on his sharp-tail and prairie chicken harvest envelope before turning it in with wing samples of both species.

*The author and his German shorthair Shani take a
breather and examine a young sharp-tail grouse at the
end of the last day of a Nebraska Sand Hills hunt.*

Chapter 27

Pan Fish and Prairie Chickens

October 2011

I was gently reminded this past week how an afternoon's outing in the beautiful Flint Hills of east-central Kansas may or may not put more food on the table but is sure to build another good outdoor memory—to savor, to share.

After a hot summer's siege of home-improvement projects, the recent autumn-gold weather finally led me to question my priorities: I paused and admired the painting, the new carpet, the fence mending and the gate rebuilding. And then I went fishing.

More to the point, while packing the float-tube rig, flipper fins and fly rod, I was already asking myself, *Whatcha gonna do if you get to the old stone quarry in Osage County and find that the summer's drought and blistering heat have dried it up?*

So, as last-minute reinforcements, I stowed a bird hunter's strap vest, No. 6 shot shells and a recently acquired RBL 16-gauge, reassuring myself that if the rock pit produced no pan fish, there were several square miles of native tallgrass pasture between my fishing hole (or dry hole) and home that had been sustaining its share of the region's greater prairie chicken population for ages.

After checking with the landowner for fishing access and crossing a cattle guard at the entrance, I drove to the middle of the pasture and found a water level only slightly below normal in a long, squarish, six-acre stone quarry with near-vertical limestone walls on three sides. Water clarity has made this a favorite fishery since back in the 1960s, just a few years after stone taken from it was used to complete construction of a nearby stretch of interstate highway.

A fly rod, tiny popping bugs and a float-tube rig help the author trick scrappy rock-quarry pan fish like this colorful pumpkinseed.

During my first five-minute drift on the breeze across the pit toward a submerged rocky drop-off, two fat green sunfish were tricked into engulfing a 64th-ounce weighted feathery thing with red head, black body and white feathery tail. Nothing happened throughout a repeat drift. But a slow paddle along the vertical limestone north shore was pleasantly interrupted by two scrappy half-pound bass that slurped and dunked a brown, fuzzy popping bug; after that, the brightest orange-bellied pumpkinseed with fluorescent blue-green streaks along its gill covers ripped the line sideways with a force belying its 7-ounce mass.

Then Mother Nature's silent alarm triggered an abrupt end to my segment of the day's solunar fish-feeding schedule. Repeated casts with a variety of flies, feathers and bugs around the edges of increased vegetation that came with the pit's drought-lowered water level produced no more interest in my offerings.

A short paddle back to the truck, fish released from live basket to strike another day, gear loaded and secured, and a quick stop back at the farmer-host's house gave me a chance to say thanks for the first half of the afternoon's therapy.

Ten minutes back along the route toward home brought me to the gate of one of those tallgrass pastures that contain just enough patches of the hated invasive *Sericia lespedeza* to attract grasshoppers and other insects—prime source of nourishment for fast-growing young prairie chickens. This was my fourth sashay of the early 2011 chicken season into the region's fenced sections of native grass.

The rancher from whom I'd secured permission to hunt had assured me that a month before he and his crew had seen a good number of young birds during a midsummer transfer of cattle to other pastures. My first three visits since the mid-September opener had produced only out-of-range flushes of several birds—probably spooked by my overhyped Shani, the shorthair project dog, who had clearly been deprived of a real hunt for too long, much like the rest of us.

However, on this day, because I'd elected to do the float-tube fly fishing first, Shani was left at home in her kennel—thereby challenging me to a much lengthier solo walk, crisscrossing the western half of that square-mile pasture from the north gate toward an old, nearly dry pond in the southwest corner. Perhaps because I was advancing steadily into the face of a south breeze without the benefit of the dog, the first prairie chicken flushed right to left directly in front of me and well within range.

The 16-gauge side-by-side snapped to shoulder and did what causes me to think it so sweet, dropping the bird in knee-high grass some 25 yards out. On the more leisurely circular hike back to the north gate with a tender young chicken for the table, several more birds were flushed, but the 16-gauge remained silent, affirming the notion that while one bird for the season is enough to fill my bag limit, there appears to be good breeding stock as we move through to winter, and as Mother Nature smiles, ample birds should be left for next year's production.

As you contemplate your next trip afield, consider packing gear for more than one outdoor objective—whether it's a fishing/hunting combo, camping/hiking/photography, or just soaking up what your available waters, woods and upland have to offer. With little fuss you can double your pleasure.

Connecticut Shotgun's RBL and a 1-ounce 16-gauge load of No. 6 shot proved an effective match for this greater prairie chicken, which bore feather patterns consistent with a young bird from that year's hatch.

Chapter 28

Hunt and Fish the Edges

October 2010

Picture this moment from your early years of fishing: You've tried several baits and/or numerous artificial lures on a beautiful day, casting into a favorite stretch of "fishy" water with little or no results. This continues to the point where the day's outing is wearing thin and you're getting a little bored. Perhaps you're suddenly tired, thirsty or hungry. You reel in the line with the intention of calling it quits when at the very instant you start to raise the rod and lift the business end of the line out of the water's edge—*wham!* Your lure is smashed 3 feet sideways and the biggest bass you've seen all summer, maybe all year, has snapped the line. Lure and fish are lost.

It doesn't take much experience for anglers of all ages to learn that 15 to 40 feet of fishing line has a whole lot more s-t-r-e-t-c-h and flexibility the instant after you cast out a lure and begin your retrieve than that same line has when you've reeled in all but 3 feet of it. So if you'd reeled in nearly all of your line and that monster described above struck your lure or bait at water's edge, I know the feeling. I still remember that "*pling!*" sound that left me staring at limp curls of monofilament at the end of my undressed line—and I can recall that queasy feeling in the pit of my stomach.

Likewise, through your years of (and lessons in) upland hunting, did you ever walk unproductive miles of grain stubble or native pastures until your feet and legs were so rubbery-numb that you shuffled birdless back to your vehicle? And then, just as you were standing around, reviving yourself with thermos coffee, pulling burrs out of your pant legs, or stuffing bird dogs and zipped-up gun cases in the luggage compartment, did you watch, slack-jawed, as a pair of cock pheasants or an entire covey of quail burst from the weedy road ditch within 20 paces of where you stood?

Now for the final exam question: What's the critical common ingredient in both of the haunting memories described above?

My guess is some of you have figured it out. Maybe you were lucky enough to have a dad, grandpa or other outdoor mentor. Or, like so many others, you've learned it with patience, persistence and the hard-won humility of trial-and-error outdoors.

What I'm talking about here is a basic concept in the ecology of small- and big-game hunting and fishing: the edge factor.

Ask any successful fresh- or saltwater angler: During the key feeding periods of each day, fish activity increases as each species moves in its travel and feeding lanes among various kinds of habitat cover. And most of those travel lanes are along or very near the borders or edges that separate one kind of cover from another.

Consider a local Flint Hills example: Watch anglers who're really good with a fly rod or spinning tackle as they work the shoreline of a farm pond, watershed lake, or even the deeper pools along a stream. Most of them use chest waders or float-tube rigs to station themselves a few feet out from the shoreline. Then they cast flies or lures just outside and parallel to the outer edge of vegetation in the shoreline shallows.

Whether fishing from a boat or a bank, during feeding periods in the early morning, the late afternoon or the evening, try casting fly or lure at sharp, shallow angles from the shoreline, just a few feet beyond any fringe of vegetation.

You see, the fish you'll be trying to catch spend a fair amount of their time each day (and night) patrolling what anglers call "structure": those visible and invisible submerged irregularities or edges where the little fishes they like to eat hang out.

Young hunters, come November or December, if an experienced bird hunter invites you along for a pheasant or quail hunt, use this experience to become a good observer; watch hunters and dogs that spend most of their time working the edges of fields—those boundaries between the birds' food supply and their weedy, brushy and/or marshy escape or roosting cover.

Oh sure, those opening weekend mega-drives with long lines of hunters and dogs sweeping across vast fields of Great Plains milo stubble can kick up dozens of hens and rooster pheasants. That kind of circus has its exciting moments. But once the bones of your Thanksgiving turkey or pheasant have been picked clean, a lot of the most satisfying upland action happens when hunters work in small groups, pairs or even solo—sometimes after a skiff of snow has brushed the landscape. And much of the cover they and the game prefer is edge cover—along hedgerows, weedy terraces, field borders, brushy ravines or stream banks.

A recent example: Just last week, on the next-to-last day of the early split season for greater prairie chicken, neighbor Bill Hartman—who's taken many species of fish and game throughout America—rolled the first pair of prairie chickens of his life out of a cloudless Coffey County sky. Both birds were flushed from the edges of lush green, insect-attracting patches of cool-season grasses and forbs scattered across a square mile of greenish-brown native warm-season grasses. And minutes before, we'd watched as a dozen or more chickens rose from under our German shorthair Shani's solid point just beyond the upwind edge of another deep-green patch.

What's going on here is repeated over and over in food chains and food webs throughout much of our natural world. Use this edge factor to become a smarter, more resourceful hunter and fisher. Become a lifelong learner and respecter of the game you pursue. Harvest only each day's fair share. Learn of ways you can help improve and maintain good natural habitat so future generations can continue to enjoy their own personal edges in our Flint Hills outdoors.

The classic mixed-grass and weed strip on the left provides great edge habitat between creek and field for game and nongame species.

Chapter 29

Year-Round Thoughts on Upland Bird Seasons

Early November 1989

The Kansas pheasant and quail seasons open next weekend. You are allowed to harvest four cock pheasants per day, and the daily limit on quail is eight. Seasons on both birds run through January 31 of the new year.

State Wildlife and Parks surveys don't paint a very encouraging pheasant picture for north-central and parts of northwest Kansas. The quail data are more encouraging, with most sections of the state expected to have populations equal to or above the 10-year average.

Those are the facts. But the facts don't begin to tell the whole story. Hunting the "big three" of upland game in Kansas (quail, pheasant and greater prairie chicken) involves much more than swinging a shotgun and pulling the trigger at just the right point in space and time to drop a bird out of our wide-open sky. The tradition means many other things:

- There are those year-round trips to the veterinary clinic to keep favorite Brittanys, Labs, pointers and setters happy and healthy members of the family.

- Kansas quail and pheasant hunting also includes the excitement that Dad feels as he stands in front of the mailbox at the end of a country lane on a July Saturday and unwraps his copy of John Madson's book "Out Home" or the latest issue of Shooting Sportsman or Gray's Sporting Journal.

- You may be the first member of the family who gets a fresh twinkle in the eye just because autumn's first morning frost has to be scraped off of windshields—a happy harbinger that the upland bird seasons can't be far away.

- Maybe it's the added intensity your dogs pour into their daily runs in the chill of a crisp October morning. These are surely not the same sluggish animals that favored shady naps through July and August.

- Upland hunting means enduring mischievous grins and verbal barbs from outdoor friends who delight when you miss a few more sporting clay targets than you expected during a preseason practice session.

- Upland hunting includes staying in touch with farmers and landowners. It means getting involved with wildlife conservation groups that raise funds locally and use them locally to improve habitat on area farms and ranches. Talk is cheap, but bird hunters can follow through by helping with tree plantings, by root plowing next to (instead of bulldozing!) a vital strip habitat of hedgerows, by reseeding erodible acres back to native warm-season grasses, and by paying a farmer to leave a few rows of milo or soybeans standing unharvested to help game and nongame species through the tough winter months.

- Hunting upland birds is steeped in tales of seasons past, skillfully spun by weathered veterans gathered around a glowing fireplace on the eve of an opening day while wide-eyed youngsters listen—and ask important questions.

- It's the tossing, turning restlessness with which all hunters, young and old, try in vain to catch some sleep in the wee hours of opening morning.

- It's the breathless excitement with which a 12-year-old comes to the breakfast table (an hour early!) on the day of her first quail hunt. She is fully dressed in gumboots and coveralls and impatiently wondering, *Why is everyone taking so long to get on with the program?*

- Hunting pheasants is watching in disbelief and amazement as that beautiful long-tailed, cackling rooster flies on unscathed by what you thought to be two perfectly placed ounce-and-a-quarter patterns of No. 6 shot from your brand-new Benelli 12 gauge.

- And it's watching with indescribable pride as a teenage son folds his first-ever pheasant out of a southwest Kansas sunset and kneels as he takes it from the one Brittany from your kennel that needs and enjoys the moment as much as your son does—with all the misses and miles of a long, hard day afield already fading into perspective.

- Hunting quail means the challenge of breaking in a new pup that occasionally waits until he's smack in the middle of a covey to slow down or to act like he senses why you brought him along. But of course that's the same pup that whirls and locks on point 20 yards downwind from a wild plum thicket and holds that point long enough for your daughter to step in for her baptism by an exploding, buzzing cloud of quail wings.

- Hunting upland birds means graciously accepting, with just the right touch of modesty, the slowly broadening smiles of surprised delight and the stream of compliments from December table guests who had no idea "wild game birds" were so delicious!

We've barely scratched the surface of what it means to hunt prairie chickens, pheasants and quail here in Middle America. This we believe: Our upland game-bird heritage is indeed infinitely greater than the sum of its parts.

Part Five: Early-Winter Overview

'Tis the season for tossing and turning through sleepless nights before opening days for the "big three" of upland birds in the Great Plains. November gives us chances to conduct on-the-ground assessments of the validity of all those prairie chicken, pheasant and quail forecasts we've been reading in newspapers, outdoor-magazine columns, state fish and game websites and media releases or watching on outdoor sporting television.

November and December provide opportunities to partake of nature's smorgasbord based on the year's actual production. Whether or not this year is a good one for us and for the game, we can always find the time, the money and the sweat equity to give something back to our hunting and fishing hosts—the keepers of the landscape—and to the habitat they maintain for all those game and nongame critters that enrich our lives.

For a more authentic and revealing account of the antics on an all-too-typical quail hunt, don't miss chapter 32, written from the bird dog's perspective!

Chapter 30

Prairie Chickens Expose Our Best–and Less Than Best

November 1984

Harold Thomsen was convinced this was the optimum hillside for us. It was half an hour before sunrise on the first Saturday in November 1981. Harold and one of our mutual hunting and fishing partners, Dale Hogan, plus my high school freshman Chris and I had parked our vehicles just minutes before in the predawn cold, a half mile north of that hill.

We quietly scattered ourselves along the west border of a bluestem pasture, snuggling down in tall grass but looking up with increasing frequency at the faint lightening of the eastern sky.

Behind us lay a 40-acre field of freshly harvested soybeans. And that was important.

Through alternate mornings and late afternoons of the previous week, Harold and Dale had been scouting a large flock of greater prairie chickens that had been flying out of the large pasture in front of us to the east and flapping and gliding to feed in the soybean stubble directly behind us to the west. So both men felt confident that positioning ourselves along this hilltop strip of tall grass between the birds' pasture roost and their morning's breakfast was our catbird seat, the place to be for some classic open-prairie pass shooting.

Prospects for that year's season had been cautiously publicized as "pretty good." Sure enough, even before it seemed light enough to see chickens from our excellent vantage point, we began to hear scattered shots in the distance, to the north and the east. I glanced to my right and watched Chris, eyes scanning the eastern horizon. Beyond him, 40 yards farther south, I could just faintly see the heads of Dale and then Harold, silent sentinels kneeling in the tall grass.

Then, in the growing light, I thought I saw Harold making a slow but deliberate hand signal toward the southeast. As my eyes shifted in that direction, it took a second for them to adjust to the sharp contrast between brightening sky and dark earth. Then I saw them, almost imperceptible at first—a flock of some 20 prairie chickens. They seemed a long way off initially, flying in a northerly path parallel to our short, thin line of predawn soldiers. But suddenly, almost as if they were being reeled in on a string, the birds circled left and directly toward our position.

Unless you're a dove, waterfowl or prairie chicken hunter, it is probably difficult to understand the level of judgment and self-control involved in knowing just the right instant to single out the image of one bird, raise your shotgun to your shoulder while you click the shotgun's safety to the "fire" position, track your bird's flight path to establish a slight lead, and pull the trigger—especially when the birds are whizzing almost directly overhead.

Sure enough, these 2-pound prairie grouse still surprised us with their speed. Some of our shots brought a bird down, and some blew invisible holes in the sky, probably several feet behind their intended targets. Dale's beautiful old setter Spot retrieved Harold's chicken and then found a bird that Chris and I both swung on at the same instant—more than 30 paces beyond where I'd marked it down.

Just minutes later, a second, larger flock came in, flying just as low and just as fast as their earlier cousins. Again, we dropped a few—Chris making a clean kill with an overhead passing shot that required a longer lead—and we missed a few more.

Just as suddenly as it began, it was over.

Dale clearly earned the "top gun" badge for the day with a classy double taken the hard way when, from that last flight coming toward us from the east, the lower barrel of his Beretta nailed an incoming, full-grown hen and then, with a graceful 180-degree pivot belying his 70-plus years and chronic hip trouble, his top barrel dropped a tender young bird of the year, going away, a 34-step retrieve to the west.

As we stood admiring our birds, Dale and Harold took time to show Christopher the distinguishing feather patterns of male and female as well as of adult and young chickens. And it was equally pleasing to hear my son's thoughtful follow-up questions.

No, not all of us had limited out. But yes, we had some good luck, some good shooting and some gratifying dog work. Except for Dead-Eye Dale, we didn't shoot so well that we could spend the next few days bragging about our performance. Yet we enjoyed the fast action enough to store up a few classic Flint Hills upland bird memories and start planning for more—next weekend, next month, next year.

Less than an hour after we'd shuffled out of our vehicles in the dark, we were back in them, rolling toward Dale's kitchen for hot coffee and his beloved Betty's cinnamon rolls.

Chapter 31

Reverberations from the Sound Track of a Daybreak Chicken Hunt

November 1988

There are nearly a dozen of us scattered out along a weedy Coffey County, Kansas, fence line. The predawn darkness prevents us from seeing even the next hunter down the line. Yet, through the stillness of a frost-covered morning, familiar opening-day-for-prairie-chicken sounds begin to emerge.

There's the muffled click of a car- or pickup-door latch—that would be the company laggard, the one guy in our outfit who is always late to the opening-day 5:30 a.m. breakfast—or misses it altogether. So he's a few minutes tardy to the remote pasture fence line that we'd agreed upon last night over slabs of pork ribs at Guy and Mae's in tiny Williamsburg, Kansas.

Are we upset with him? No. He's the chap who spent every sunrise of the previous week scouting and confirming another season's legal access to hunt this stretch of landscape. He's our farmer/host's neighbor: one who can be trusted to bring hunters who respect this privilege to harvest a native chicken or two as they fly across the land in their low-altitude, flap-flap-flap-flap-glide route toward breakfast in nearby soybean or grain sorghum stubble.

There's the unmistakable sound of a long zipper against the backdrop of an eastern sky that is beginning to take on a pink tint. The hunter next to us is either losing an outer layer of coveralls because it is 15 degrees warmer than last night's weather gurus predicted, or there's an urgent need to lose some of those extra cups of breakfast coffee from Linda's Café in Lebo.

A rooster crows from the barnyard to the east of us, announcing the beginning of his day.

From the Topeka hunter to our left comes the trademark sliding, clicking sounds of a favorite pump shotgun, followed by the equally familiar sounds of two or three more shells being pushed into its tubular magazine. Oh well, it's encouraging to know somebody remembered he could remove the plug after last week's goose hunt.

The rooster crows again, heralding advancing streaks of light from the eastern horizon.

We can see three hunters down the line now. The nearest two are squinting eastward, watching for the appearance of a cluster of tiny, silent specks they hope will grow closer against the dawn.

For what seems like enough time to risk dozing off, we hear only the sound of our breathing against the morning chill. Then the report "A flock of 20 or more off to the northeast!" comes relaying down the fencerow in excited, coarse whispers.

A riff of weeds and tall grass rustle as nervous, excited hunters rise to their knees, watching intently as the cluster of specks slowly, steadily grows in size and nearness, transforming into familiar silhouettes in flight.

We hear a whole scattered row of shotgun safeties click from the "on" position to "fire!" and the whistle of air through pumping-gliding-pumping-gliding wings—but still well out in front of us.

A premature single shot rings out from far down the fence line. Was it from the beginner's 20-gauge owned by the neighbor kid, overanxious on his first prairie chicken hunt? Or was it the expensive over/under 12-gauge of his uncle, an equally excited Kansas City dentist?

The morning sky erupts in gunfire followed in the growing light at close intervals by the sight and the sound of soft thumps of 2-pound prairie grouse hitting and rolling on damp, frosted pasture grass.

And enriching this treasured tradition as always, there's the muffled sound of short oaths and looks of amazement and growing respect from the eyes of some who turn and follow the majority of the flock as it escapes untouched to the west.

Then there is the sound of controlled pride in the voice of the veteran hunter who quietly accepts compliments and slaps on the back for scoring a double. He bends at the waist to accept his wheat-colored Lab's retrieve of the second bird; and there's the language of teasing among lifelong friends—who saw other friends swing gun barrels on passing birds and miss clear, open shots as cleanly as they themselves had.

Finally, there's the hissing sound of a coffee thermos and a tin of homemade oatmeal cookies being opened and shared all around by those who join in this mud-caked SUV- and-pickup tailgate celebration of another autumn opener for tallgrass upland birds.

Season's greetings!

Chapter 32

Happiness Is Quail Scent: From a Brittany's Perspective

November 1972

Author's note: This tale has been adapted from an outdoor column originally appearing in The Emporia Gazette in mid-November 1972 and written by author Scott Irwin. In the weeks that followed, the revision presented below seemed necessary to get the story straight, as told from the point of view of its real hero— me, promising young Brittany Reverend Busby's Buttons, just plain Buttons to you folks and to my master, this book's author, and to the nice old professor, Dale Hogan, who is owned by my mother, Busby's Becky. She and Dale gave Scott the pick of Mom's first litter—me, naturally.

*

I'd been flaunting birdy, "Quail alert!" body language for a full minute. If my master and our favorite field companion, retired professor Dale Hogan, from nearby Neosho Rapids, had been a little more alert, that first covey of the season might not have gotten off so easily.

There I was, not yet 2 years old, and locked in a solid point downwind from a dense clump of buck brush (coral berry). Dale was positioned behind me and to my right, working his way through a stand of sumac. He took a noisy step closer, and 15 brown-feathered blurs erupted with that hauntingly familiar explosive buzzing sound that only a nice healthy covey of quail can use to shatter creek-bottom silence (and nerves) on a frost-covered morning. Sound familiar?

When this first, less-than-graceful encounter was over, my hunters offered a pair of predictable excuses: "There I was, two steps short of getting out of that bloody thicket when the covey flushed," moaned Dale. "The first (and only) shot I got off was rudely interrupted when the swing of my gun barrel was stopped cold by a sumac branch! My only shot was probably 6 feet behind the last bird to leave the area."

Meanwhile, Scott offered a plaintive nugget when he whimpered, "I had just straddled the fence and was making sure to push the top strand of barbed wire down far enough to swing my trailing leg over when—aw shucks—I was sorta facing away from all of you and hadn't even noticed Buttons was on point."

Sound familiar?

You nonhunting readers wouldn't believe what we bird dogs have to put up with—especially on the first few quail hunts each autumn. And this example represents what happened a mere 10 minutes into the edge of an ideal upland bird habitat: a beautiful quarter-section of patches of grain sorghum (milo) stubble broken up by woody ravines, brush-lined ditches and fenced borders, and two small parcels of native bluestem hay meadow.

Just moments earlier, with a reassuring scratch behind my ears, Scott released me from the old dog box in the back of Dale's brown Chevy pickup. This was our first encounter of the year with the gentleman Bobwhite Quail. And that opening comedy of errors is probably more typical of early-season tactics than some quail hunters would like to admit. Yet Dale and Scott didn't seem particularly disturbed by the incident.

But why should they be? I may be approaching the ripe young age of just 2, but they already know they can count on me. Plus, when that first covey flushed, Dale and I were in a better position to notice that most of the birds settled right back down in a little thicket a hundred-plus yards straight ahead of us.

As the three of us approached more good-lookin' cover, I quartered toward the downwind edge and almost immediately picked up that heavenly scent again. And with the previous episode fresh in my memory, I struck an unusually high-headed point—my way of signaling, "Heads up, guys! There are quail somewhere in front of us here." But I'll be danged if five or six of those feathered speed merchants didn't flush wild just before my hunters had moved into ideal position.

As luck would have it, the birds sprang from the far-left side of the plum thicket and Dale couldn't even see them. But Scott was more focused this time and dropped one of the birds. I marked it down and was released to retrieve it. Just as I picked up the quail and turned to deliver it, a straggler bird flushed late and curled right back over the top of the brush patch. Dale made a nice gun mount and swing of his Beretta over/under and rolled that beautiful little rooster into the edge of the milo stubble.

With a flair belying my youth, I graciously dropped Scott's bird at his feet on my way to retrieve Dale's bird to his outstretched hand—as if to say, "Nice shot, old fella." In fact, Scott added his approval by praising me with a couple of pats on both of my shoulders and turned to ask Dale, "What have you heard from the other buyers of Button's litter mates? If they're as pleased as I am, this has to be a win-win-win situation for everybody." I tried my best to give 'em a modest lookin' "aw shucks" blush.

After a brief examination of those first two fat healthy quail, my hunters agreed we'd scattered that covey enough. It was time to turn to other cover. With the scent of birds from that covey freshly reprinted, the day got more tantalizing. Ten more minutes and 200 yards up a gradual slope of the landscape, I sniffed that delicious scent again.

Unfortunately, my beloved guys were lagging behind (still babbling over my previous performance, no doubt) as the aroma of quail increased with each of my silent steps forward. With surrounding vegetation so dense the guys couldn't see my staunch point, the largest covey of the day blew out. Birds were flying in almost all directions but mostly out of range and out of my shooters' view.

No shots were fired; in fact, none of us could see beyond the cover to tell how far and in which direction(s) the majority of those quail had escaped.

We had just caught our breath and then pressed on past a giant cottonwood, turned to the east and were approaching another plum thicket stretched out along an old, slumping fence when a wave of bird scent slammed me with such intensity that I whirled my head and neck at a right angle to my body and froze in a distorted, crouched point.

Both hunters were paying attention this time. Scott explained later that he was about to signal Dale to come toward him to get a better angle for shooting but he never got the chance. A single quail that burst out of a clump of short grass had been creeping along ahead of me until I altered my twisted point to take one more step. Through a curious repeat of unfortunate circumstances, Dale was not standing in a safe position to shoot. Scott was seemingly the man with the luck thus far. His 20-gauge spoke sharply, and the bird tumbled in knee-high foxtail grass 25 yards out. I nonchalantly found and delivered the bird, got an appreciative pat from my master and we moved on.

Working our way forward with Dale and Scott on opposite sides of the plum thicket fence and me leading the way, moving back and forth working the breeze, we traveled maybe another 30 yards when another single bird burst from the grass directly under Scott's feet, hooked sharply back to our left and outmaneuvered the shot string sent after him.

Scott shuffled along a few more paces, muttering to himself about not staying alert. (I must admit there are times when I wonder if he's becoming too dependent on me and my pedigreed sniffer.) He had just started mumbling yet another lame, whimpering plea for attention and sympathy when a third single popped out of the grass. This one must have moved a little more slowly, because my master pivoted, shouldered his 20-gauge and swung through the bird's line of flight, and the under barrel's seven-eighths-ounce shot string patterned the bird convincingly.

During my modest retrieve I was thinking, *This should pretty well cheer up the old guy and convince him I've justified at least another month's high-performance food and an insulated dog barrel with front-door weather flap.* Sure enough, when I deposited the bird at the toe of my master's old Redwing lace-up boot, he said, "Good dog, Buttons!" and enthusiastically stroked my shoulders, which seemed to perk things up for everybody.

We crossed a fence bordering another part of the milo stubble and worked our way along opposite sides of a weedy, brushy ditch. With this kind of quail habitat, plus the months of training during my rookie season, I felt pretty confident I'd find a new covey any moment.

Another hundred yards along the ditch, a shift in the breeze coming from my right brought that unmistakable fragrance! I bolted 50 yards into some uncut milo whereupon my abrupt halt and crouched point spurred the hunters into action. Scott crossed the ditch and joined Dale as both walked toward my now-solid point.

Nevertheless, for the third time that morning, the birds flushed before my guys could get into position. But even quail can make mistakes in their escape routes. Most of this covey flushed right back over my shooters' heads, and Dale dazzled us with a magnificent, fast-swinging double: Two shots and two birds fell, while the survivors blew 150 yards right back down the ditch we'd just hunted.

I had to sniff around for a minute or two before finding the first of Dale's pair, and he pointed out the second bird for me—lying on bare soil between rows of milo. With both birds delivered to our proud shooter, we made our way back down the ditch in search of singles. We found fewer escapees than expected, but both hunters made nice, tough-angle crossing shots from in front of my last two stylish points.

We wrapped up a great opening day for quail with the drive home for one of Betty Hogan's legendary lunches (complete with gourmet table scraps), bird cleaning and packaging, and naps in front of a black-and-white television delivering Kansas versus Kansas State football. And the blue ribbon that tied this package into a memorable gift for me, Buttons, the proud and devoted bird dog, came in the back-and-forth excitement with which my two wing shooters described the morning's highlights for Betty at the lunch table, bragging to her about my beautiful and reliable sporting dog work.

As I reflected on the day's good fortunes, it was encouraging to note how well Dale Hogan handles the encroaching limitations of his advancing age—especially considering that this 70-something bird hunter limps from a nagging hip injury suffered in his high school football days and survived a cardiac event and subsequent bypass surgery a few years ago.

Though I'm guilty of struggling with my youthful impatience and with straining to hunt at ramped-up speed, Scott has coached me to adapt our strategies—for everyone's benefit—when Dale is with us. If the landscape and cover on a given day are a little more challenging, we hunt about 200 yards at a time; then we pause, give Dale time to catch his breath, to regain circulation and to lose the tingling sensation in that cranky hip before resuming our moderate pace.

That approach seems to bring out the best in all of us: I have more time to scent birds, we seem to walk past fewer tight-holding singles, and my hunters are more relaxed and better prepared to be in optimum shooting position when my sniffer locks down on birds.

None of us has reached perfection afield. But the affection and respect we feel for each other and the birds we pursue sure make this bird dog feel appreciated.

Chapter 33

Who Says Texans Cain't Hunt Like Gen-a-muns?

November 1983

It was only minutes before straight-up noon and unseasonably warm for the second Saturday in November. Three of us were hunting a triple line of trees that formed a shelterbelt along the back border of the house and lawn of our host—and my old high school friend—Ed Hesser, on his southwest Kansas farmstead.

We were approaching the tag end of the tree line. The most imposing cover in front of us was a ridge of head-high tumbleweeds wind-drifted against a fence.

Just beyond Ed's machine shed and livestock pens, we'd been crisscrossing his "home" quarter section of milo stubble all morning with good success. We'd been sufficiently busy bumping and occasionally bagging cock birds that flushed mostly to our north and east. So even though we hadn't seen any pheasants double back behind us to the south and slip into that levee of weeds stacked up against his shelterbelt, decades of memories of these long-tailed, multicolored kaleidoscopes and their clever avoidance schemes led us to stay on port-of-arms alert.

As we drew abreast of the last tree in the shelterbelt row and stood stock-still for maybe four seconds, less than a hundred yards facing away from the back-door entrance to Ed's farmhouse, the north end of that berm of tumbleweeds exploded!

Pheasants, mostly hens, burst out in twos, threes and scattered singles. Fred Crawford was a step in front of Jim O'Leary and me. That's where he wanted and needed to be—and it paid off.

With that trademark nerve-jangling cackle, the first gaudy rooster to burst from the cover had barely cleared the top of the tallest weeds when Fred's 16-gauge Ithaca pump gun spoke a single, terminal "*thwump!*"

The grin on the face of my West Texas friend seemed permanently fixed. "That does it, y'all," Fred said. "Yeah, not a bad mornin's work," offered Jim. I looked at my watch. It was 12:02 and we had filled our limits of four cocks each.

The full effect of that morning's success blends in my memory like a collage:

- The heavy frost we scraped off of the windshield of Fred's motor home while Jim cooked our predawn breakfast.

- Those opening-day butterflies that knotted our stomachs until the second and third hens used their free passes* to flush untouched, silhouetted against the sunrise.

- The strategy we improvised for hunting the four corners outside the perimeter of one of Ed's half-mile-diameter center-post irrigation circles—with two of us zig-zagging back and forth across the corner stubble while the third man skirted ahead and blocked the far point.

- And who among us could ever forget the shot with which Jim bagged his fourth bird—deftly executed when we took a midmorning breather for thermos coffee and oatmeal cookies? While lighting his pipe, Jim was rudely interrupted by a cock that sprang from a road ditch immediately beside him! He

---

* Kansas and most pheasant states restrict the harvest to roosters. Hens are protected.

calmly repositioned the angle of the pipe stem in his teeth, shouldered his Browning 20 and made the rest look easy.

- The special satisfaction that crept over us as we admired Fred's last bird and walked through the rusty gate into Ed's backyard.

- The leisurely lunch, spiced with joking and teasing about some of our more spectacular misses of the morning.

- Saving the longest tail feathers as we cleaned and iced the birds through the midafternoon in the shade of an elm beside the old machine shed.

- The arm twisting it took to get our host to join us in our celebration over cold beers and a rib-eye steak dinner in Garden City.

- Not believing the opening day's almost hot, shirt-sleeve weather—even when the evening weather guy on the radio in the motor home told us that all-time-high November temperatures were recorded all over the Great Plains that day.

In any case, we were on an all-time high of our own, induced by a career day with Kansas ring-necks.

I had talked with Fred and Jim in previous years about coming up from their homes in Odessa, Texas, for a try at our long-tailed birds. They'd generously shared some great dove and blue-quail shooting with me during the eight years in the 1970s when I'd lived and taught at a small university in the Permian Basin oil country. But 1980 was the year we got it all sorted out.

While I've returned to my native Kansas to live and to teach at a university there, during several Novembers since then, Fred, Jim and I have enjoyed a similar retreat, sometimes with the addition of one or more of our sons.

To be sure, the birds have been tougher to fool some years than others, and those deep furrows between rows of irrigated milo and corn stubble seem just ever-so-slightly tougher to walk each autumn.

Funny thing, though: I have experienced very few kinds of fatigue more gratifying than that coming at the end of such golden days as November 12, 1980, when I hunted with such treasured friends.

So here we are, and our gentleman friends the bobwhite quail and the ring-neck pheasant have issued still another invitation to the sporting harvest of their surplus production. We'll interpret the renewal of your Kansas hunting license as a positive RSVP. Good hunting.

The 20-gauge in this photo and the out-of-his-mind-lucky guy hanging on to it for dear life throughout the morning hours of a Kansas pheasant opener have probably never had it so good—before or since!

Chapter 34

Nonstop Laughs Flavored with Incidental Pheasant Hunting

November 1988

Jim O'Leary leaned his lanky Texas lawyer's frame back into the overstuffed easy chair, filled his pipe with a favorite blend from an old leather pouch, lit it with several unhurried puffs, stroked his overstuffed midsection and asked, "What is it they say in that old '70s beer commercial? 'Boys, it just doesn't get any better than this.'"

We were sprawling in the lobby of a Garden City steak house, celebrating another memorable opening day harvest of upland bird royalty—ring-neck pheasants.

Fred Crawford—Odessa, Texas, lumber and hardware dealer and full-time sparring partner of O'Leary—quipped, "Don't pay any attention to Jim. He's just in mild shock from baggin' his first limit of pheasants without falling down, stepping in something or shooting at least one hen."

Jim's quick counter in deep-voiced drawl was typical: "Fred, your ego's just smartin' from watchin' that rancher's 12-year-old kid fill his limit before you dropped your second bird! And by the way, I thought we'd explained to you on the drive up through the Panhandle about those black-colored birds." Jim turned to my son Matt and me and in a tone of mock indignation asked, "Do y'all have any idea how embarrassin' it is to have a member of your own huntin' party deliver three pheasants and a *crow* to the Sublette locker plant for processin'? I'll bet that sweet Mennonite lady at the counter is still laughin'."

Just because we were hosting these two old friends from the West Texas oil patch didn't mean we were immune to their barbs. During the dessert course of our meal, Fred winked at Matt and then glanced at Jim long enough to say, "O'Leary, nudge the great outdoor scribe over there and let's see if he's awake—ur, uh, make that alive! Did y'all ever see anybody so out of shape? Whadda you do to get into condition for the upland bird season, Irwin—lift extra rations of Twinkies?"

And so, friends, another opening day chasing the western Kansas ring-neck pheasant drew to a close. As we've driven back to our home following several of these November reunions, I've never been sure if we're more exhausted from following dogs and roosters across the vast irrigated croplands of Gray and Haskell counties or from 48 hours of almost nonstop laughter.

In retrospect, I think it's the latter; the sometimes great, sometimes so-so bird hunting is just bonus.

*

Postscript: After a successful career in West Texas corporate law, Jim O'Leary retired; he and wife Diane moved to Austin to be nearer to his children and their families; Jim died in 2007.

Fred Crawford divorced, sold his Odessa lumber and hardware company, remarried some years later and moved to a prime location, centrally situated among several golf courses southwest of Fort Worth.

Edward Hesser, our host landowner for those annual reunion hunts, had been a happy-go-lucky, hard-charging three-sport letterman on our tiny southwest Kansas high school's teams in the 1950s. Ed lost the family farm in 1984 to the same relentless inflationary conditions that had wiped out several neighbors within the same five-year span; he worked for a few years as an OTR agribusiness trucker before dying of the same stresses and coronary disease that had taken his father.

Chapter 35

The Birds Are There, but Young Legs and a Good Dog Help

Late November 2012

You'll need young and/or superbly conditioned legs and lungs to find quail (or pheasants) with or without a good bird dog in the habitat-challenged landscape over much of Kansas this year. Did we mention it'd help to be young?

Last weekend, the opener for quail and pheasants, we were in Nemaha County, northeast Kansas. The quail were there—in some of the same hedge-and-locust fencerows and along some of the same creeks as in past years. The habitat was drought-stunted in this landscape. Yet our dog did all we could ask. When quail were found and pointed, if we didn't get on the birds quickly for the initial flush, forget it. They were across the road or fence and into inaccessible timber in four seconds flat!

Walking on a gimpy knee didn't hamper Bill Hartman's wing shooting on opening morning. With the smooth-pumping Winchester Model 12 20-gauge passed down from his father, he took three quail from the first covey we sampled along a wooded ravine that angled across corn stubble.

When he dropped the first one, our shorthair Shani was on it and halfway back to me with the bird in her mouth when a late straggler flushed on Bill's side of the tree line. At the instant he shot this second quail, Shani dropped his first bird on the leafy turf, deep within a dense plum thicket she was threading her way through, and backtracked to Bill's side in search of the second bird.

Both of us watched with fascination as she found the second quail and brought it about halfway back to me, dropped it in a shallow gully, and returned to the dense thicket where she picked up Bill's first bird. Shani brought it out of the heavy cover and, with a trace of hesitation, laid it two steps in front of me. Since I was on the opposite side of the brushy ravine from Bill, I pocketed his first two quail in my game bag. Half a minute later Shani was acting "birdy" again as she worked through some clumps of grass between us and then froze on solid point.

Two quail burst from cover. One flew straight through trees and brush so thick all I could do was watch the blurred action over the top of my shotgun barrel. But Bill was fast on its partner, and just as the bird crossed the gully between us, he rolled it from the air to a feathery stop in a small patch of bare earth 15 steps in front of me.

Walking back to the truck, old quick-draw me thought, *This is an interesting gig; I haven't fired a shot yet and there are three quail in my hunting vest.*

After a cup of thermos coffee and a few home-baked cookies, we relocated about three miles to the Nebraska side of our host's family farm. We worked Shani back and forth along a mile or more of meandering grass and forage strips intersected by a beautiful tree-lined but drought-withered creek with no flow and only a few scattered pools separated by gravel bars and beaver dams.

No birds—quail or pheasant.

Shani was gradually becoming more interested in the treetop squirrels we kept stirring; Bill's knee was beginning to bark at him; and both of us were imagining our host, Jim Harter, ringing the noon dinner bell from the back porch of the family farmhouse a half mile south.

So we decided to skirt the south and west borders of an 80-acre Conservation Reserve Program (CRP) field on our way back to my truck. Just as we approached a minimum-maintenance dirt road, Bill spotted a major covey of quail settling into a grassy, weedy cover strip bordering a creek a hundred yards in front of us. Shani tiptoed in, went on solid point and held it.

What we had failed to notice when the covey settled into that cover strip was that three or four outliers had glided a little farther along to a lush patch of still-green clover a few paces to our right. So, in what was supposed to be one of those "Kodak moment" scenes, Bill and I walked in and concentrated on the cover to our left in front of Shani's point.

You guessed it: Our vintage tableau was shattered as the unnoticed quail quartet to our right exploded from its hide, prompting young Shani to break her point. This caused me to yell, "Whoa!" a split second after Bill's first shot fluffed one of the early risers. My "Whoa!" command to the dog distracted and slowed his swinging on a following bird.

We'll never know whether Bill's first shot or my shout at the dog flushed the main covey to the left. All I can report is that my one and only shot of the day was very flustered and very late (well into wing-and-a-prayer range) and didn't rustle a single feather as the greater part of that beautiful covey scattered across the dirt road and vanished into a neighbor's off-limits timber beyond.

After a restful lunch break and a 40-wink nap, we walked a few more creek-side grassy strips and one pheasanty-looking brushy draw leading to a nearly dry farm pond—but to no avail. By midafternoon, the day was darkened by heavy cloud cover, the wind was howling a gale from the northwest, and Bill's left knee was convincing him it would be more comfortable supporting him in his extended practice of the culinary arts. (Translation: It was his turn to fix supper.)

Just for the record, Bill Hartman is a skilled wing shooter and at least as good a chef, and he did not disappoint on this 2012 opening weekend. And, as is often the case, after the great food and rich, hearty, laugh-filled conversations with our host and friend, Jim Harter, a two-hour drive home was made easier by more rich conversation. There was a bonus this year: a special stop at an Amish country store one mile north of Sabetha for a healthy variety of baking, cooking and nibbling delights.

On reflection, all of these pieces are parts of another opening-day patchwork quilt of memories that is the priceless and durable fabric of upland hunting. The hunting part of the trip would most likely have been hard, birdless work without our unpolished but eager dog. We hope your season is off to a bird-, friend-, and dog-enriched beginning.

Neighbor, friend and accomplished fly fisherman Bill Hartman
is almost as fine a wing shooter as he is nonstop entertainer
and hands-down top chef in any hunting or fishing camp.

Chapter 36

Outdoor Thanksgiving

November 2011

Since this is the season for counting our blessings, I'd like to consider some outdoor gifts for which I am indeed thankful.

While the summer of 2011 initiated a drought most of the Great Plains and the Southwestern states would like to forget, I'd still like to offer a relieved "thanks" to Mother Nature for providing a few recent rains and some of the best fall fishing, camping and hiking weather in memory. Until the current cold spell, I was still catching nice stringers of pan fish on a fly rod, casting from a float-tube rig on area watershed ponds. Through how many late Novembers can you remember catching pond bass on spinners and bait-casting lures?

I'm thankful for the delightful days of fishing, hunting and just walking the land with a number of new and old friends of retirement age. Their quiet wisdom, nurtured by decades of outdoor experience, inspires me to redouble my efforts to invest in the future by sharing my outdoor life in these Flint Hills with more youngsters and their families.

A nod of appreciation goes out to all the wildlife conservation organizations and agencies that serve us. (See appendix.) In this time of shrinking budgets, there are ever-expanding challenges to do more with less. The Kansas Department of

Wildlife, Parks and Tourism continues to have courteous, tireless and dedicated professionals working for us and our wildlife.

The next time you enjoy a duck or goose hunt (or even reminisce about one from years past), don't just thank a local member of Ducks Unlimited for all the organization has done to preserve, expand and develop wetland nesting and brooding habitat throughout North America, but join the group and help the ducks for your grandkids' enjoyment. If my mental math is right, Ducks Unlimited is approaching its 75th year of service.

I'm equally grateful to all the other area conservation groups—those working on behalf of quail, turkeys, pheasants, deer and elk—and to all their members who work so tirelessly on fundraising, habitat enhancement, wildlife education, ethical sport hunting, and firearms safety for numerous youth groups.

And who wouldn't be grateful for the generosity of area organizations, businesses and individual citizens whose financial support has resulted in the recent expansion of facilities and programs with great staff and volunteers at nearby Camp Alexander and Camp Wood?

Semi-finally, I remain eternally thankful to those patient, long-suffering, good-natured farmers, stockmen and landowners without whom we simply would not have outdoor sports to pursue throughout these Great Plains. I thank every hunter and angler who has made a resolution to share his or her properly cleaned and packaged wildlife harvest with landowner hosts. It's the least we can do for the privilege of enjoying that harvest.

Finally, all of us who hunt and fish are forever indebted to equally patient spouses, family members and significant others in our lives who find their own creative ways to fill the hours while we recharge our psychological batteries afield. So, spouses, know this:

The time we spend outdoors does not mean we love you less. But if some of us didn't spend time outdoors, relieving the stresses of day-to-day living and regrounding our sense of place in the larger web of life, we'd probably be less lovable, less loving and less appreciative of all the things you do that enrich our lives.

Happy Thanksgiving!

Chapter 37

Same (Drought Blues) Song–
Next Verse with Nebraska Birds

December 2012

Beyond the similarities between recent bird hunts in east-central Kansas and south-central Nebraska, the differences provided by a recent trip to the latter—both predictable challenges and limited spurts of success—were in the devilish details.

Kevin Church of rural Emporia and I took a couple of days after Thanksgiving to return to the tiny, country-crossroads hamlet of Huntley, Nebraska (population: 40-something) and its surrounding loess hills, creek bottoms, brushy draws, and grain fields. We hoped for a repeat of the last few years—a sporting chance for pheasants and quail.

We'd made all the usual arrangements by e-mail and cell phone with one of Harlan County's deeply rooted livestock and row-crop producers. This is the same farmer who, when we first met him in 2007 in Huntley's 10-by-15-foot self-service coffee shop (next door to the farmers' co-op), scanned a detailed map of the county I'd bought from a Huntley Lions Club member a couple of years prior. That was before the club's shrinking membership forced the 2011 cancellation of a half-century-old local tradition: the annual pheasant hunters' map sale that gave resident and nonresident buyers access to all the local farms marked on an area map. Those community-minded landowners had donated hunting access to selected portions of their property for the whole pheasant season for $25. And for 50-plus years, that Huntley package was complete with a generous biscuits-and-gravy, pancake-and-sausage feed on the mornings of opening weekend.

While the Lions Club map was no longer legal scrip for access to that part of Harlan County, our above-and-beyond-neighborly coffee shop host studied our wrinkled copy, pulled a pen out of brown coveralls and marked for us selected parcels of his land that offered zones of upland game-bird habitat that wouldn't lead to undue disturbance for his livestock. Even with annual rotations of crops and livestock, that landowner and the map he marked have served us very well these past few years.

Kevin and I studied the map again, drove gravel roads to examine this year's upland cover and crop rotations, and chose to begin our hunt through a broad, brushy ravine that forms most of the mile-long east boundary of our host's half section of grain stubble. Heretofore, that ravine has provided textbook escape and loafing cover for pheasants, quail, turkeys, deer and countless nongame wildlife.

Not so this year.

That ravine, deep and wide enough to suggest ancient glacial activity, and several other coverts that were productive in prior years, revealed just how much drought, loss of CRP set-aside acres, and increased livestock grazing had reduced wildlife cover. Even so, five minutes out of our pickup, one flashy ring-neck burst from the far end of a short, weed-choked draw that sloped toward a nearly dry stock pond. The rooster was well out of shooting range, most likely crowded by my overanxious shorthair, Shani.

We crossed deep-furrowed corn stubble to the edge of the anticipated long, wide ravine. Fifty yards in we were surrounded by much-reduced ground cover, all of it pretty well trampled by livestock foraging.

The dogs made quartering patterns while Kevin and I worked the edges as we passed through the ravine. As a result, Kevin made a nice shot on one bird from the staggered flush of a medium-large covey of quail, nicely pointed and retrieved by Greta, his promising young shorthair.

From the far end of the thicket from which they erupted, I watched eight or 10 of the birds scatter back in the direction from which we'd come, landing in a wide-open stand of drought-stunted pasture grass. We were licking our chops, anticipating the singles and doubles that we would take over staunch points from that skimpy cover.

You guessed it: Hunters and dogs neither saw nor scented any sign of those singles during a thorough, unhurried vacuuming of the birds' landing strip or from a hundred more yards in all directions.

A longtime hunting mentor, the late Dale Hogan, used to grin and say in such situations, "Quailed again!"

We pushed through the remainder of that long ravine with just one hen pheasant flushing from her scant cover and flying to a neighboring field. (Upland game laws restrict pheasant harvest to roosters only. Hens are left to fly—and hatch next spring's chicks—another day.)

As we arrived back at the truck, the dogs pushed on a few yards and down over a pond dam we'd crossed earlier. Kevin went to the right side and I started left but dropped down to kick out some thicker grass below the old dam. Kevin and Greta were nosing around in knee-high grass 60 yards beyond me when a brassy, cackling rooster sprang up, gaining altitude in my direction.

Since Kevin's line of sight was such that he couldn't fire, it was up to me. The bird flew almost directly over and a little in front of me in a gentle left-to-right arc, the classic passing shot. I mounted my sweet little over/ under 20-gauge, swung through the bird's flight line in what I thought was the textbook butt-beak-*bang!* strategy, firing first lower then upper barrels in unhurried succession—and missed!

So, humbled but not beaten, we drove a mile or two back toward Huntley to work the dogs through isolated patches of cover dotted over three more quarter sections of our host's pastures and cropland—only to find more drought-stunted and heavily grazed habitat.

As the late-afternoon sun was sinking, we approached a broad gully meandering across a pasture we were crossing to get back to the truck and call it a day. Suddenly, both dogs perked up and assumed more "birdy" body language. Two or three quail flushed wild at the limits of shotgun range. Then, a few steps farther along, more birds burst from the scrub, and I folded one that fell right between a pair of scrawny cedar trees. Shani was on it before I pocketed the empty or reloaded.

Meanwhile, Kevin, squinting into the sun, marked a weathered old fallen tree 150 yards up the hillside where he'd seen some of the covey settle in. We worked the area for 10 minutes, but except for a couple of birds that flushed much farther up the hill, well beyond where we'd expected them, most of that covey gave us the slip. Quailed again.

The first property we hunted the following morning brightened things. We hunted grain-field borders and brushy draws and peninsulas that had not yet been winter grazed by livestock. So the cover was nearly as thick as we remembered from previous years.

Even though no pheasants or quail flushed within range throughout the first half mile, we pushed deer, turkeys, one rooster pheasant and a hen or two out of the plum thickets and giant ragweed well ahead of us.

When we reached the road bordering the north end of our field, we moved laterally over the hilltop grain stubble to our left where the dirt road made a deep cut through the next hill, creating a steep bluff that led downhill again at the next deep, wide ravine—which also contained lots of wild plum strips, sumac and more tall ragweed. Greta and Shani were just entering the heavier cover when a cock flushed from the distant bottom of the draw and disappeared over the top of another plum thicket on the far west edge.

Kevin was just topping the steep grade from the road to my right when, with a split-second's separation, two gaudy roosters launched from the near edge of the draw, accelerating low and fast from right to left. The No. 6 pellets from the lower barrel of my 20-gauge took care of the first bird, and before I could even think about the second rooster, Kevin and his Browning over/under made it look easy. Greta was on the scene and doing her best to retrieve both birds with one mouthful!

Two or three more roosters spooked well ahead of us from the same ravine, and we followed at least one back through the strip of cover from which we'd entered that field 45 minutes earlier. But the bird did what skittish pheasants do: blend silently into the landscape. So we'd been roostered again too.

We made two more uneventful passes through smaller coverts, then loaded dogs and gear and headed for our Kansas Flint Hills and home.

"Well then," you ask, "was one quail and one pheasant for each man all you garnered from this trip?" No. We enjoyed eight hours of good intermittent conversation going and coming, gained a renewed appreciation for a variety of Kansas and Nebraska landscapes, and had a great dinner after the first day's hunt. (Next time you pass through Holdrege, Nebraska, at lunch or dinner time, ask for directions to a country crossroads restaurant called the Speak Easy. Your tummy will thank you.)

Would we make the same trip again? Hmm. Drive out on Burlingame Road, northeast of Emporia, take a right at County Road 205 and go one mile east to Tallgrass Custom Wood Products. Retired wildlife biologist Kevin Church, now a sawmill owner/operator, will tell you whether he and bird dog Greta would make the trip again.

I know bird dog Shani and I will travel to Huntley again—in a heart(land)-beat!

Kevin Church praises his shorthair Greta for her
fine work with Nebraska pheasants.

Chapter 38

More End-of-Year Thanks and One More Resolution

December 2011

While driving across my beloved Flint Hills this past weekend on another return trip from surveying the quail and pheasant populations of south-central Nebraska, I thought of a few gifts for which we friends of the outdoor life might express thanks. So, even if I'm repeating myself from previous writings through the years, consider for a moment how thankful we should be for …

- The mild autumn weather we have enjoyed through many Octobers and early Novembers—extending the fishing season for fair-weather anglers and making it downright pleasant for hunters of small upland game. And likewise,

- The timely advance of damp, cold, blustery weather that has delivered migrating ducks and geese for waterfowl hunters and stirred up whitetail deer activity for the big-game crowd;

- The many species of fish and game that remain available to the average citizen—due in part to (a) friendly, hospitable farmers and landowners; (b) the majority of sporting outdoor people who display common courtesy and respect for the land, the landowners, and the wildlife we enjoy; and (c) competent wildlife professionals who guide us in wise use of our outdoor resources;

- Adults who invest in future generations' enjoyment of and support for natural resources by engaging youngsters in bird watching, camping, fishing, hiking, wildlife conservation, and hunting;

- Outdoor volunteers of all types—the hunting safety instructors in every city, town and village; the leaders and members of wildlife conservation groups such as the Audubon Society, the Quail and Upland Wildlife Federation, Ducks Unlimited, Pheasants (and now, Quail) Forever, the Rocky Mountain Elk Foundation, Trout Unlimited, the Wild Turkey Federation, and more;

- The impressive sums of excise tax dollars from the purchase of hunting, fishing and camping equipment that are returned to wildlife management budgets in all 50 states;

- Our very own Great Plains ecosystem of Middle America, with its blend of tall- and shortgrass prairie rangeland and row-crop farmland and ...

- The most faithful stewards of this land—the resident farm and ranch families;

- Bird dog pups and old pickup trucks;

- Whole generations, mostly of Brittanys, with an occasional English setter or German shorthair—all of which were forgiving of our shortcomings while making us feel good about most of them and elevating our optimism and sense of well-being;

- And last but not least, that favorite shotgun, .22 rifle or surprise birthday fishing rod and reel passed down to us by a grandfather or a special mentor.

I'll bet the farm that you have several outdoor items unique to your own "thankful" list. And you and I can resolve for the coming year to add some time, elbow grease and money to the writing and voicing of those thanks—to the sources of our many gifts.

Appendix

Selected Great Plains/State Wildlife Conservation Agencies

The quickest, most complete information about each of the Great Plains conservation agencies listed below is available through the web address listed for each; from there, you can access an impressive range of outdoor opportunities and services including online purchase of hunting, fishing and camping permits; maps; access to state parks; walk-in public hunting sites; each agency's outdoor magazine; videos, printed materials, and much more.

- Iowa Department of Natural Resources, Wallace Street Office Building, 502 E. Ninth St., Fourth Floor, Des Moines, IA 50319-0034; phone: 515-725-8200; website: iowadnr.gov

- Kansas Department of Wildlife, Parks and Tourism, 512 SE 25th Ave., Pratt, KS 67124; phone: 620-672-5911; website: kdwpt. state.ks.us/

- Missouri Department of Conservation, 2901 W. Truman Blvd., Jefferson City, MO 65109; phone: 573-751-4115; website: mdc. mo.gov

- Nebraska Game and Parks Commission, 2200 N. 33rd St., Lincoln, NE 68503; phone: 402-471-0641; website: outdoorsnebraska. ne.gov

- Oklahoma Department of Wildlife Conservation, P.O. Box 53465, 1801 N. Lincoln Blvd. Oklahoma City, OK 73105; phone: 405-521-3851; website: wildlifedepartment.com

- South Dakota Game, Fish and Parks, 20641 SD Highway 1806, Fort Pierre, SD 57532; phone: 605-223-7660; website: gfp.sd.gov

- Texas Parks and Wildlife, 4200 Smith School Road, Austin, TX 78744; phone: 1-800-792-1112; website: tpwd.texas.gov

Annotated List of Selected Commercial Suppliers of Outdoor Goods and Services

Most of the suppliers of outdoor gear, goods and/or services listed below are mentioned in one or more chapters in this book. They are listed here because they are locally owned and operated, offer fine-quality gear and honest, personalized service, and have established time-tested reputations and shop atmospheres that you'll be hard-pressed to find in the mega outdoor-supply chains. None of these suppliers underwrote this unsolicited tribute or knew they would be listed here.

- Bluestem Farm and Ranch Supply, 2611 W. US 50 Highway, Emporia, KS 66801; phone: 620-342-5502; website: bluestemfarmandranch.com. Click on the "About Us" label on the home page; the two paragraphs there capture the spirit of this place. When relatives and friends are visiting local folks from out of town or state, many won't go home until they've done another walk-through at Bluestem. Who knew a family-owned farm-and-ranch store would have a selection of fishing tackle that rivals Bass Pro and Cabela's? Give yourself a couple of hours just to give the outdoor-sporting-goods and dog-care aisles a thorough inspection.

- The Gun Den, 708 Commercial, Emporia, KS 66801; phone: 620-342-0711; website: thegundenemporia.com. Owner Chuck Fechter has modest quantity but impressive quality and variety of hunting and shooting merchandise and services. And staff archery pro Dave can custom-tailor most bowhunters' requests. Bring your sack lunch and sit around the "philosophers' table" ...

at least as long as you honor the code: what plays at this table stays at this table!

- Show-Me Gunstocks, 19557 Quail Ridge Road, Warsaw, MO 65355; phone: 660-438-4568. Owner Donnie Gemes was the custom shop foreman for Reinhart Fajen before that world-class gunstock supplier ran out of heirs to keep the family business going. Gemes bought the best of Fajen's equipment and gunstock blanks and brought a handful of master stock makers with him to establish Show-Me Gunstocks in 2001. I've finished several of Show-Me's semi-inletted stocks, had its staff do the checkering, and, as described in chapter 25, also had the shop custom-fit, checker and finish replacement stocks for a Winchester Model 12 and Model 21. The work has been excellent with a reasonable turn-around time.

- Simmons Gun Repair and Specialties, 700 Rogers Road, Olathe, KS 66062; phone: 913-782-3131; website: simmonsguns.com. Since 1945, Simmons has been a full-service gunsmithing facility that handles anything from basic repairs to complete restorations. Simmons has built its reputation on the installation of ventilated ribs on all makes and models of shotguns. The backbone of the business has been its work on Winchester Model 12s and Model 42s. Click on the web address above for a dazzling display of the range of products and services this close-knit veteran team of master smiths can provide.

- Smoky Valley Shooting Sports, 2341 14th Ave., Lindsborg, KS 67456; phone: 785-227-4318; website: smokyvalleyshootingsports. com. Although the Smoky Valley store is located four miles out in the country, south of Lindsborg, Kansas, it has a most impressive inventory of equipment and gear for all the shooting sports—maybe the best selection of bow hunting and archery products in the central Great Plains. The new and used firearms include several best-selling brands and top-of-the-line models. The store's website includes state-of-the-art videos and much more. And all this comes with a small-town, family atmosphere and personalized service.

Granny Buffon's Apple Cake Recipe (See chapter 6.)

Marguerite "Granny" Buffon (1910–2002) was a tiny little woman who spent her adult life as an infectiously happy and energetic farm wife and mother, a teacher in a one-room country school, a church and Sunday school pillar, and an all-around friend to everyone who knew her in the rural communities of Chase County, Kansas. Like so many of her peers, she was a wonderful cook. And, even though the recipe below may not be original with Granny, each fall and winter, she used the apples produced by the two small trees outside her kitchen window to their full potential, producing full stomachs and blissfully happy taste buds.

Granny Buffon's Apple Cake Recipe

Mix: 2 cups sugar
           3 cups flour
           1 teaspoon baking soda
           1 teaspoon salt
           1 teaspoon cinnamon

Add 3 cups of chopped apple, and mix into the above until coated.

Add: 1 1/2 cups cooking oil
           2 eggs (slightly beaten)
           2 teaspoons vanilla
           1/2 cup chopped nuts

Bake in ungreased 9-by-13-inch pan at 350° for 60 minutes.

Glaze apple cake with:
           1 cup powdered sugar
           1 Tablespoon corn syrup
           1 Tablespoon butter
           1 Tablespoon milk

Mix and pour over warm cake.

If you can fend off the bystanders, let the cake cool, slice it and serve pieces of a size based on the amount of love being shared or on the winning auction bid.

About Pass It On - Outdoor Mentors (See chapter 18.)

Pass It On – Outdoor Mentors is a Wichita, Kansas–based national organization dedicated to providing children with mentors who will share traditional outdoor activities with them. The group's mission is to give children opportunities to connect with nature, an experience that they more than likely won't have without a mentor showing them the way. Partnering with organizations offering similar conservation and youth participation programs, such as Big Brothers Big Sisters, the Quail and Upland Wildlife Federation, Pheasants Forever/Quail Forever, the National Shooting Sports Foundation, Delta Waterfowl, the Rocky Mountain Elk Foundation and the National Wild Turkey Federation, among others, volunteers with a passion for the outdoors can give a child the chance to fish, to hunt or simply to spend time in the fields with a caring adult.

For more information about Pass It On – Outdoor Mentors, visit www.outdoormentors.org.

Contact Information for Huge Vintage Fishing Tackle Collection (See chapter 19.)

Noel Lyons is willing to receive inquiries from anglers and tackle collectors who are seriously interested in buying major portions or, preferably, all of his collection of fishing gear. He is a true gentleman, has a great sense of humor, and has a story to go with practically every item in his second-story "museum" over a triple garage.

Readers can reach him by phone at 620-342-7649. He asks that you call in advance to schedule an appointment to see his collection.

Bibliography

Basket, Richard. "Ecology and Management of the Mourning Dove." Edited by Mark Sayre, Roy Tomlinson, Ralph Mirarchi, and Thomas Basket. Harrisburg, Pennsylvania: Stackpole Books, 1993.

Hill, Gene. "Mostly Tailfeathers." New York: Winchester Press, 1971.

Irwin, Scott (aka Masche Field). "Flint Hills Outdoors," Emporia Gazette, 1972–2014.

Kavanaugh, James. "Walk Easy on the Earth." Kalamazoo, Michigan: Steven J. Nash, 1991.

Leopold, Aldo. "A Sand County Almanac." New York: Oxford University Press, 1949.

About the Author

About a decade into a 47-year career that saw him teach high school biology and coach track and field and then instruct aspiring science teachers at the university level, Scott Irwin began writing about his other life.

Irwin says that he was "lucky enough to have been born the last of eight children, raised in post-Depression years in two Kansas towns—both small enough that the common existence for families included having some combination of big vegetable garden, hen house, small barn, milk cow, and house and lawn chores that instilled an early hands-on work ethic."

But there was always room to explore the wild things.

From early childhood, Irwin was schooled by older brother Jim in small-water (pond and creek) fishing and then as a hunter of backyard "spatzies"—armed first with a slingshot fork carefully crafted from a box-elder limb with just the right symmetry and powered by pre–World War II red-rubber inner-tube strips and later with a Daisy BB gun.

By age 12, Irwin was stalking cottontails and squirrels with his dad or the Hogan brothers, using his father's vintage Springfield .22 single shot. Oldest brother Jack gifted him with a tack-driving Remington 511 bolt-action .22 with a five-shot clip, and Irwin thinned out the jackrabbits that swarmed southwest Kansas during his 1950s high school days.

Carpentering with his father's building crew and then working part-time jobs during college, Irwin was able to purchase a Winchester Model 12, and a new realm of wing shooting enriched his outdoor sporting life. These pursuits have continued in seasonal cycles through marriage, family, graduate school, a distinguished public school and university teaching career and, in 2009, retirement.

A chance 1972 conversation between Irwin and retired banker Bob Foncannon, who'd stepped down after many years of writing a weekly outdoor column for The Emporia Gazette, led to an interview with editor Ray Call and sports editor Jim Nirider. Four editors and at least a dozen sports editors later, Irwin has built a 42-year archive filled with good, bad and ugly accounts of things "outdoor wild" across the Kansas Flint Hills—with seasonal forays into Nebraska, Missouri, Arkansas, South Dakota and West Texas.

This book, "An Outdoor Sporting Life," presents a reflective sampler from those years.

Scott Irwin is a native Kansan, a retired university professor,
a lifelong fisher of small waters and hunter of upland birds
throughout the Midwest and the Southwest. He has written wildlife
conservation articles for The Emporia (Kansas) Gazette since 1972.